THE GIRL
SLEUTH

THE GIRL SLEUTH

A Feminist Guide

by
Bobbie Ann Mason

421877

The Feminist Press
1975

Manufactured in the United States of America.
Composed by O. B. U., New York, N. Y.
Printed by the Faculty Press, Brooklyn, N. Y.

Library of Congress Cataloging in Publication Data
Mason, Bobbie Ann.
    The girl sleuth.

    Includes bibliographical references.
    1. Children's stories, American—History and criticism.
2. Girls in literature. 3. Detective and mystery stories,
American—History and criticism. 4. Bibliography—
Children's books issued in series.
I. Title.
PN1009.A1M32   813'.0872   74-22313
ISBN 0-912670-17-7

Cover design by Gilda Kuhlman

For my parents

Contents

Preface

A WHILE BACK I was in graduate school, studying literature and various schools of criticism, researching the sources of *Ancrene Wisse* and debating the meaning of Stephen Crane's "red wafer" in the sky (was it a communion symbol, a lollipop or merely the sun?). During those years I never heard a soul mention mystery novels. Or science fiction stories. Presumably no one even remembered that he or she had once read the Hardy Boys and Tarzan and Tom Swift and Nancy Drew. For that matter, I don't believe anyone even mentioned the words tree, butterfly, cat, or clothes line, to give a few typical examples, unless they occurred in a poem. And then we didn't talk about actual trees and cats, but only about metaphorical ones.

After I put the finishing touches on my dissertation—on Vladimir Nabakov, that wiley master of artifice—I settled, in a stupor, into an old habit I once had. Reading. Fast reading. The kind where you don't get up from the chair until you finish the book. And soon I had gravitated toward my favorite childhood stories, series books about daring girl detectives who solved mysteries and herded gangs of crooks to justice.

I soon found out I wasn't alone. A lot of literary critics are transferring from the traditional areas to study the influence of popular culture. Scholars are now publishing articles on heroes such as Archie Bunker and Nero Wolfe and Humphery Bogart. Some critics today are studying popular culture, devotedly, for its own sake; some perhaps for escape; and some are studying it because for better or worse popular culture is important to people. It reflects our real desires and values and it helps mold them.

Certainly most children have preferred the heroes and heroines of the mystery and adventure series books to the characters in their grade school readers and even to the protagonists of force-fed classics. However, histories of children's literature have systematically ignored the existence of series books. Critics of children's literature have dismissed them as bad habits. Elementary education textbooks used in colleges have made only passing reference to them.

But the fact remains that girls and boys love them and have read them voraciously for decades. By applying critical tools to these books, we open new ground in a manner which I find doubly affirmative, for it gives the study of fiction a new relevance and, more importantly, it acknowledges signficant textures of our real (if sometimes embarrassedly hidden) lives. Some critical judgments made about popular novels, movies and songs will be postive, some negative; but in a basic sense the entire undertaking is positive in that it helps us to discover who we really are—an essential prerequisite to deciding who we want to become.

Since I am interested in the heroines, I will try to question here why girls so eagerly follow the pursuits of girl detectives such as the Dana Girls, Judy Bolton and Cherry Ames. What is in these books that holds a girl between nine and fourteen spellbound?

It is my purpose to give some critical attention to the form and substance of some of the series books which girls read, to comment on their quality and their possible impact on young girls' imaginations, and to examine the stereotypes which have been popularized by the books.

After all, Lolita must have read Nancy Drew and the Bobbsey Twins. We all did.

Acknowledgments

I wish to express my gratitude to the following persons who were sources of information and encouragement for this project: Harriet S. Adams, Arthur Prager, Margaret Sutton, Julie Campbell Tatham, Helen Wells, and Lee Zacharias.

THE GIRL
SLEUTH

The Aunt Jane's Nieces Series

BOOKS FOR GIRLS BY EDITH VAN DYNE

SEVEN TITLES

Aunt Jane's Nieces   Aunt Jane's Nieces at Work
Aunt Jane's Nieces Abroad   Aunt Jane's Nieces in Society
Aunt Jane's Nieces at Millville   Aunt Jane's Nieces and Uncle John
Aunt Jane's Nieces on Vacation

Distinctly girls' books and yet stories that will appeal to *brother* as well—and to older folk. Real and vital—rousing stories of the experiences and exploits of three real girls who do things. Without being sensational, Mrs. Van Dyne has succeeded in writing a series of stories that have the tug and stir of fresh young blood in them. Each story is complete in itself.

The Aunt Jane's Nieces series (advertised here on a 1909 book jacket) anticipated the growing market for books about girls who had adventures. Eventually the adventurous heroines of girls' series became detectives.

1

Clues to the Girl Detective

·When I was six or seven I read my first novel—*Honey Bunch: Her First Trip to a Big Fair.* Honey Bunch was a Shirley Temple of a prig-nosed little girl with grown-up manners and goldilocks, and she never got her chambray and challis dresses dirty. "Honey Bunch," says the book's blurb, "is a dainty, thoughtful little girl, and to know her is to take her to your heart at once." Honey Bunch was so sweet and perfect that I despaired, but no matter—Honey Bunch was out to see the world and I wanted to tag along. The Big Fair was miles bigger than any little Kentucky county fair I had ever seen (with limp 4-H Club vegetable displays and a glittering midway of Gypsy hawkers and gaudy machines that whirled through the air), and it enthralled me. Honey Bunch and her parents rented a cottage near the Big Fair and stayed two months in order to see all the exhibits. And while she was there, Honey Bunch got mixed up with a bunch of Eskimos and solved a mystery.

From there, it was only a few Christmas presents to the Bobbsey Twins, charming children who captivated me for several years with their perfect lives, a contrast in every way to the paltry, dull life I felt I led. The

Bobbsey Twins were never punished and they were allowed to travel and solve mysteries; they didn't live on a remote farm where you had to feed the chickens and milk the cows every day. When the Bobbseys did travel to the country, they found a paradise of woolly lambs and fragrant haymows and pretty red barns and gentle ponies—no mud or bugs or sun-blistering chores. Their free delight reinforced my conviction that my family was isolated and deprived, and created fierce longings for travel and adventure and middle-class comforts. The only place I knew where people had central heating and their own bedrooms and vacations was in the Bobbsey Twins books.

There was more in store. If Honey Bunch and the Bobbseys occasionally solved a mystery, there were other characters who spent all their time hot-footing it after clues. I read them all: Nancy Drew, Judy Bolton, Beverly Gray, Kay Tracey, the Dana Girls, Vicki Barr, Cherry Ames. I was an authority on each of them. But they were also *my* authorities, the source of my dreams. The ideas I derived from them and carried to adulthood (you only have to imagine me lugging these dreams on the train to New York City when I left college) were that the art of living was to be like a girl detective and that New York was the center of the universe. A girl detective was a sort of tourist out to see the world and solve its mysteries, bringing back souvenirs of the solutions, little picture postcard proofs of adventure, the real life.

There was something about the dawn of the decade of the 1970s that made grown women and men suddenly dig up their old Nancy Drews and Tom Swifts and start devouring them like starved adolescents with a pile of dirty books. When I found my worn copy of *The Secret in the Old Attic*, hidden in my attic since 1952, it was the beginning of a luxurious lapse into my past. I eagerly resurrected all my old series books. What an unfathomable delight to discover my childhood heroines, to let drowned memories come surfing back, to be a child again and know what I know now! What a slave I was then to the Bobbsey Twins! How I had longed to solve mysteries with Kay Tracey and Judy Bolton! How I had admired Nancy Drew for her cleverness and poise and freedom! As I read these old books, itching to write about them, some little voice told me I wasn't originating a new pleasure but sharing in a cultural discovery. And, in fact, Nancy Drew and the Bobbsey Twins and Tom Swift and the Hardy Boys and all their friends are all over the place these days in a new wave of nostalgia. Scholars are poring over them as if they held the keys to the cabala. Rover Boys and Ruth Fielding books are collectors' items. I saw an old Buck Rogers priced at $18, and an original Superman comic was sold for about $1,800 last year. A man in Iowa quit his university professorial position just so he could have time to study this whole scene. The Modern Language Association (the august MLA!) scheduled a seminar on juvenile series books at its 1973 convention.

There are several things this popular culture movement legitimizes: it says it's okay for literate people to like kitsch; it's okay to revisit your childhood; and it's okay to be scholarly about both. We are seeing the emergence of the Scholars of Relevant Trivia. Skeptics may scoff at their embrace of our shabby society, and to an extent the craze may be an anti-intellectual over-reaction; but a lot of this current energy, I think, is a positive recognition and understanding of our sources—a better motive than adolescent rebellion or snobbish intellectual isolationism. Feminism can partake of this energy in a healthful way by juggling critical perspective with some honest enjoyment of our personal histories.

Where would women's liberation be without Nancy Drew and Judy Bolton and Beverly Gray and Cherry Ames? Nancy Drew alone has been crucial to the lives of millions of girls (no one can count how many) since 1929 when the first Nancy Drew mystery, *The Secret of the Old Clock*, appeared. She was the first official girl sleuth, and the rest came tumbling after. The fact that these heroines of adolescence were teenage detectives with unusual freedom is important to feminist consciousness—for better or worse. We've come a long way from Nancy Drew, but there are many adult women walking around with images of her—in a neat blue suit, driving her blue roadster—tucked down close to their hearts. Nostalgic affection for the girl sleuths abounds. Nancy Drew even has a fan club in California, a band of adults who stroll Memory Lane together in quest of clues to their past. The influence Nancy Drew has had is complex, and perhaps serious, as I began to realize when I read *The Secret in the Old Attic* again.

I will look closely at the individual girl detectives in later chapters. First, I want to show where the girl sleuth came from and what kind of reading background sends little girls in the direction of mystery-adventures. Mysteries are the favorite genre of both sexes (the Hardy Boys are the most prominent of the male detectives). The form is borrowed from adult detective stories, and while children's mysteries too stress a strong sense of justice and social order, they aren't whodunits—for murders are taboo—but adventures. Girls' books, especially, use the trappings of the mystery genre—crooks and clues and gothic settings—to glamorize the trespass into adulthood. Boys' books tend to have more action and less mystery, but boys have other adventurous roles as well—jungle explorer, inventor, soldier, athlete. Girls, even those who have careers (nurse, reporter, airline hostess), act principally as detectives in girls' series books. Why is solving mysteries the special domain for girl adventurers in fiction? And have these "liberated" heroines liberated their readers?

In the first three decades of this century, series books were big business and new series came and went like hit songs do now. Grosset & Dunlap, Inc., A. L. Burt Co., Lee & Shepard, Street & Smith, Inc., Saalfield, and Cupples & Leon Co. were among the big publishers. Most of the companies are now defunct and their juvenile titles long out of circulation, but Grosset & Dunlap continues to issue old faithfuls like the Bobbsey Twins and the Hardy Boys. The series books in their heyday were a commercial phenomenon, but what was most phenomenal was that so many of them were written by syndicates that cranked out children's books on an assembly line. The authors of many well-loved series weren't flesh-and-blood humans, but pseudonyms for ghost groups. A child never knows that, and it's shocking to learn it even as an adult. Imagine a row of writers in a desk-filled room. They have just punched the time clock, their old black Royals are cleaned and synchronized—ready-set-go! They type in syncopation and a copy-person doles out the parts, the chapter outline and quota for the day. Of course, they didn't operate quite like this, but my sense of betrayal makes me picture them this way.

Most of my early childhood favorites came out of Stratemeyer Syndicate in East Orange, New Jersey, a group which has unquestionably had the greatest influence on American children's books.[1] Since 1910 Stratemeyer Syndicate has originated over a hundred series, totaling more than 1,200 titles. Most of them have been published by Grosset & Dunlap, while the syndicate owns the properties and gets the royalties. I still haven't recovered from my astonishment at learning that one man was responsible for creating so many of my old favorites—Honey Bunch, the Bobbsey Twins, the Hardy Boys, Nancy Drew, Tom Swift. Edward Stratemeyer, the wizard at the wheel of this most famous fiction factory, dispensed his series in all directions, like tentacles, to nearly two dozen publishers. Until he died in 1930 he churned out children's books at an unimaginable rate. His head was so overflowing with ideas that he couldn't write books enough to contain them, so he circulated three-page plot outlines among staff writers, who filled in the details for a flat fee—$50 to $250 per book, with no royalties or other rights. Stratemeyer published over 700 books under approximately 70 pseudonyms—cryptic names such as Ned St. Myer and E. Ward Strayer, as well as upright Hollywood names—Jim Bowie, Hal Harkaway, Roy Rockwood. The talented Garis family worked closely with him, writing hundreds of Uncle Wiggilys, Tom Swifts, Bobbsey Twins, and many others. Roger Garis, in his reminiscences of his days as a syndicate staff writer, wrote:

> I think we all enjoyed writing for Mr. Stratemeyer. We lived the characters, even though they were for the juvenile market. It is amazing how excited one can get saving a character from the Caves of Ice, with a whole tribe of Indians about to attack.[2]

Garis said Stratemeyer was "a slender, middle-aged writer with tremendous drive, imagination, and a remarkable business sense." Stratemeyer was also keenly attuned to what turned children on, and he gave them the action-jammed adventures of ideal, wholesome, all-American characters who lived in perfect places. His own favorite was the Rover Boys, a series he wrote personally, with love.

Stratemeyer, who was a disciple of Horatio Alger, won respectability for his low-priced fiction by putting his series books in hard covers, distinguishing them from the ubiquitous "dime novels," of which he had written plenty. But he couldn't stop librarians and English teachers from getting upset over the wild adventures of his immensely privileged and precocious characters. The leader of the Boy Scouts thought these books were too stimulating to the imagination and, moreover, they pictured children doing forbidden adult things! Actually the books were outrageously wholesome and strictly moral, and children loved them. "Our big success has been to let the young heroes do the doing, and to keep adult interference to a minimum," says Andrew E. Svenson, a present syndicate partner. That success has been virtually immeasurable. Twenty million copies of these "fifty-cent juveniles" had been sold by 1930, and Grosset & Dunlap still sells five million copies annually at three times the price. Harriet S. Adams, Stratemeyer's daughter, manages the syndicate and personally tends to the Nancy Drew series. A small staff continues to pen Tom Swift Jr., the Hardy Boys, the Bobbsey Twins, and the Dana Girls, the best-sellers which have survived the realities of social change and the video distractions of cartoons, cowboys, and comedians.

Critical histories of children's literature carefully omit references to the popular series books of the twentieth century, as if their uncomfortable presence could be wiped out of history in the same way librarians ban them from their shelves. They are absent from educators' textbooks. But the sentimental nineteenth-century series books, such as Little Prudy and the Five Little Peppers, are granted respectability. Louisa May Alcott's famous *Little Women* was also part of a series, begun at the request of a publisher who wanted a girls' series to rival the popular Oliver Optic boys' books of the mid-nineteenth century. *Little Women* inspired girls' fiction for years, but it took decades for writers to create descendants of the true heroine of that book, Jo March, a tomboy with a chestnut mane, a rebellious girl who became a symbol for a growing restlessness among females.

At the turn of the century (after decades of Little Prudy and Elsie Dinsmore and Pollyanna) there was an evident need in girls' fiction for action, accomplishment, exhilaration—inspiring challenges that would promise identity in the world outside. Amy Bell Marlowe's "Books for Girls," a Stratemeyer series, were "somewhat of the type of Miss Alcott," according to the ads, and they often focused on an individual girl's brave struggles. Another turn-of-the-century series, Aunt Jane's Nieces, by Edith van Dyne (not a Stratemeyer pseudonym), was about "girls who do things," according to one book cover. It was about time girls did things, and Edward Stratemeyer saw to it that they did—in fiction at least. There was a growing market for female adventurers, and eventually the girl detective emerged as the most "liberated" and celebrated of heroines.

At first girls did things in groups. It was safer. In a group they could do what they didn't dare do alone. The Bobbsey Twins were one of Stratemeyer's first successes in this category. The series, by "Laura Lee Hope," appealed primarily to very young girls, and after it became popular Laura Lee Hope's name was tacked on like an appliqué to three series for older girls—the Outdoor Girls, the Blythe Girls, and the Moving Picture Girls. Group heroines began to proliferate in the juvenile book industry—the Adventure Girls, the Khaki Girls, the Linger-Not Girls, the Blue Grass Seminary Girls, the

Meadow Brook Girls, the Motor Maids, the Motor Girls, the Girls of Central High, and several varieties of Girl Scouts and Campfire Girls. Many individual heroines were actually surrounded by sidekicks and sororities. These "modern" girls wore khaki knickers and climbed trees, rode horses and rowed boats. Some of them went to war. They often exhibited uncommon bravery and maturity, and they sometimes solved minor mysteries. They were credited with uncovering crucial clues, performing amazing rescues, or revealing uncanny intuition. And at night these healthy heroines donned their starched frocks and danced.

If it hadn't been for the automobile and the airplane, the girls might not have gotten very far. The Motor Boys series was tremendously successful, and Stratemeyer Syndicate, quick to flaunt the taboo of the woman driver, conceived the Motor Girls in 1910. "No one is better equipped to furnish these tales than Mrs. Penrose, who, besides being an able writer, is an expert automobilist," said the ads. Mrs. Penrose was also one of the many pseudonyms spilling out of the syndicate. The Motor Maids, a competing series, appeared in 1912, and the Bluegrass Seminary Girls puttered about on "motorcycles." The auto also provided the allure of independence and mobility to the Automobile Girls and the Meadowbrook Girls. The Outdoor Girls—who were capable of cross-country hiking and camping—drove around casually, to the awe of some of the girls they met.

"Do you mean you drive around all alone?" she asked, her voice a little awed.

"Suppose you have a blow-out?"
"That's easy," laughed Mollie. "Ask us a hard one. If we have a blow-out or a puncture, we fix it, or use the spare."

These heroines were "liberated," for they didn't wear
bustles or look generally helpless and they could set out
in their cars to do whatever they had a notion to do.
The Outdoor Girls piloted their own cabin cruiser,
rescued drowning sailors, and won boat races. As long as
they were in a group they needed no role but that of
pleasure-seekers, sharing the illusion of emerging eman-
cipation.

These groups of girls had their weaknesses, however,
the major one being romance. The girls weren't truly
independent, for their money came from Daddy and
their main interest was boys. They were almost
invariably upper crust. Many of them spent a good deal
of time chattering and stuffing themselves with chocolates. They made fudge while their boyfriends tracked
down scoundrels. It was permissible for girls to find
clues and ask questions, and even to perform various
secondary heroics, but not to catch thieves. (Catching
thieves is man's work!) At Wild Rose Lodge, a quaint
cottage in the country, the Outdoor Girls were
frightened by an inhuman monster (King Kong or his
cousin) in the woods and were too terrified to go
swimming. If only the boys would come, they would
know what to do! Then the boys came (on leave from
the war).

If these dainty adventurers weren't being chased by a sleuth of bears or bogeys, they were being captured by Gypsies or thieves. The impulse for heroics was strong, because the dangers to the gentle sex adrift in the world seemed enormous. Daringly, girls not only motored unchaperoned—they flew their own airplanes. Spectacularly, once one airplane got off the ground, the air was populated with fictional girl pilots. It was a significant over-reaction: as soon as there was an opportunity, girls literally flew out of the house. Edith van Dyne wrote the Flying Girl series about self-reliant Orissa Kane who flew a tinker-toy contraption with paper wings (in about 1911), and proved "resourceful and plucky" by rescuing her reckless pilot brother. Girl parachutists and aeronauts claimed several series, and eventually most girl detectives could fly solo when the necessity arose, although the more recent Vicki Barr series has reduced the airborne heroine to a stewardess in a trim blue uniform.

The chronicles of sewing bees, the perils of the debutante, and romances at boarding school were too dull, so many of the new series were advertised as "modern" and "up-to-date." On the other hand, there was danger in allowing girls to become airplane pilots. In the boys' series, the heroes were on a single-minded mission to become manly. But there was no way a girl could rack up exploits in any heard-of role that would be ultimately acceptable to society. The series form demanded adventures, or episodes, or continuing exploits, but the ordinary life of the female had three episodes: menstruation, marriage, and motherhood. The individual adventurous heroine was slow to evolve because it was risky to let a female strike out on her own—and succeed. An extraordinary kind of heroine was required, one who would enthrall with her

Edith Van Dyne's Orissa Kane was one of the first girl aviators. According to this 1906 ad, the Flying Girl "proves resourceful and plucky, and saves the day in a most thrilling manner." Commercial aviation later produced the hostess heroine who solved mysteries in the sky.

glamorously interesting life, but who would not, of course, encourage revolution, since women had virtually no legal role or opportunity outside the home. The auto and air girls were perhaps false steps on just this count. There was, after all, the cooking to be done. It turned out that mystery stories best suited the necessity for thrilling girls safely—teasing their desire for adventure without threatening the comfortable advantages of femininity. By solving mysteries girls could confront the unknown with ease. The sleuths were aided and abetted by males and money; and their readers could aspire toward this thrilling paradox of adventure and security. It was pure escapism for the readers, since no one solved mysteries or had such adventures in real life.

With the increasing independence of the heroines, there emerged a strong mystery pattern. Actually, from the beginning of series books there were slim mysteries about orphans and family secrets and inheritances and hidden jewels and suspicious scheming "sharpers." By the 1930s, solving a mystery had become an established plot formula for both boys' and girls' series, and in girls' fiction the focus gradually narrowed to a single sleuth (brave and plucky, keen and crafty, nosy and shrewd) on the trail of a gang of crooks. Ruth Fielding was the most outstanding of these prior to Nancy Drew, but her popularity declined after the war—and her marriage. She was a modest, poor orphan who worked her way toward fame and fortune in the films. The series at first dealt with her spirited struggles against adversity, but adventure and mystery popularized the series when sentiment wore thin. Then in 1928 there appeared the first girl sleuth (who was called one) that I have been able to discover: *Bobs, A Girl Detective*, by Carol Norton (published by A. L. Burt Co.). Bobs' achievements were meager: she failed at three cases, which managed to get solved without her cleverness. But although this book has less unity than almost any book I have read (and popular juvenile books are exceptional for their unity, even though they were sometimes written in several sections by separate writers), Bobs was a refreshing personality, an independent girl who went out into the world to work as a detective. She was a "hoidenish young girl" affectionately called "Bobsy" by her sisters, but in the end she traded her magnifying glass for True Love.[3]

There is no clear sequence to the development of the girl detective heroine, but when Nancy Drew drove her blue roadster onto the scene in the early 1930s the public was ready for her.

> The driver, a pretty girl of perhaps sixteen, attractive in a frock which either by accident or design exactly matched the blue of her automobile, smiled whimsically.
>
> *The Mystery at Lilac Inn*, p. 1

Nancy was popular precisely because of this blue car, which carried her into more dangerous situations than usually graced the pages of girls' books. (In some volumes she drives a "sporty maroon roadster," and readers have always been impressed with the way she backs her car "skillfully" out of her driveway and "maneuvers" into tight parking spaces.)

Here there was a deliberate focus on an unusually strong heroine, far more accomplished and independent than any of her predecessors. Nancy Drew was more liberated than girls had dared imagine—as free and self-possessed as any adult. With her success, the amateur girl detective became the staple heroine, and it was a magical role if there ever was one. Sleuthing was something a pubescent could identify with that was radically adult; it provided the promise of something beyond domesticity. Girl sleuths from all directions followed Nancy Drew's trail. Career girls who solved mysteries on the side sneaked onto the scene—nurses, journalists, even movie stars. Bonita Granville, Jane Withers, Ginger Rogers, and Tillie the Toiler lent their names to Whitman editions in this decade. All of these new heroines were principally sleuths, regardless of their ostensible roles (and there were more careers open to women in the 1930s and 1940s). The day of the girl groups tooling around to escape boredom was over. The new heroines were serious-minded and independent. Moreover, they tended to get older and their readers younger. Outside of mysteries, there were only a few mushy romances on the market. The new focus was on an individual consciousness—one extraordinary girl in the act of solving a mystery.

Most of the girl detective books that followed were written by "real" authors, but often on commission for a publisher who decided that a nurse series, for example, would make money. Most of the authors, subsequent to Stratemeyer, were women, but they adopted the commercially successful pattern he helped to create.

It remains for the academicians of popular culture to document the sources of the girl detective. It is not my purpose to provide a detailed history, but to offer some interpretations of a few of the major girl sleuths, to see if I can suggest why we loved them and how they have affected us. How are women to interpret these popular heroines now? How "liberated" were these independent and intelligent adventurers? I will try to give my version of these problems by telling about my own experience in reading and following the trail of these alluring girl sleuths. First I read Honey Bunch and the Bobbsey Twins, and then I graduated to the incredibly adventurous girl detectives, who carried me well beyond adolescence. They loom large in my legend and in those of countless women. How must we face them again?

HONEY BUNCH FELT VERY IMPORTANT AS SHE GOT ON THE TRAIN.

Honey Bunch: Her First Big Adventure.   *Frontispiece (Page 7)*

Honey Bunch was Shirley Temple's literary precursor portrayed and illustrated as a dainty stereotype—clean, obedient, cute, talented, and usually much more careful about her dress blowing in the wind. In later books of the series Honey Bunch was a detective.

2

The Land of Milk and Honey Bunch

Honey Bunch was my first friend in fiction. She offered me tantalizing glimpses of the outside world. Honey Bunch: Her First Auto Tour! Her First Trip West! Her First Trip in a Trailer! Her First Trip to the Big Woods! Her First Little Mystery!

Honey Bunch toured the world but all the time she watched over her dolls lest her children be naughty or spill something. She played tea party with her mother, pretending the milk was tea and the cookies were "charlotte russe cream puffs." She was mother's little helper, learning to bake a pie, wash her dolls' clothes, and sweep under the bed.

> Some little girls I know do not dust the lower shelves of the tables in their houses. They think that no one can see the dust there. But Honey Bunch was not like that.
> *Honey Bunch: Just a Little Girl*, p. 151

Honey Bunch was the perfect little Miss Priss.

When I was a little Honey Bunch I started writing my own novels (Bobbie Ann: Her First Little Novel). I remember asking my Granny, "How does a writer think up a whole book? Does she just make it up as she goes along?" My Granny allowed as how Laura Lee Hope (the Bobbsey Twins) and Helen Louise Thorndyke (Honey Bunch) got the plots all worked out in their minds beforehand; they made plans, they didn't just write the first thing that came into their heads.

Edward Stratemeyer's Sunny Boy series (by "Ramy Allison White"), books for very little boys, preceded Honey Bunch. Sunny Boy, whose Aunt Bessie calls him "honey-bunch," is decidedly more child-like than Honey Bunch, who is a five-year-old grown woman. Instead of playing tea party, Sunny Boy pretends he is a general commanding his army. And the book jacket describes the series as the adventures of a "little fellow with big eyes and an inquiring disposition, who finds the world a large and wonderful thing indeed. And somehow there is lots going on when Sunny Boy is around. Perhaps he helps push! . . . He learns a lot and he helps a lot, in his small way." Sunny Boy makes up little songs to amuse himself and turns somersaults on his bed. I don't believe Honey Bunch ever turned a somersault. Honey Bunch learned to sit quietly, with her dress smoothed neatly (how can you turn somersaults if the sky will fall in should anyone see your panties?), or to stand demurely, left hand on hip, wagging a reproving finger at a naughty little boy with a frog in his fist. She learned to be, in fact, a juvenile Victorian matron. Honey Bunch books, read by girls between six and eight, lay the foundation for sexual stereotyping in books to be read later. Edward Stratemeyer profoundly understood the market value of the stereotyping of the sexes. It's as plain as pink and blue.

Honey Bunch thinks baby pigs are homely and she hates bees and finds dead fish dreadful. She helps her mother keep the "naughty weeds" pulled. She is capable and serious at age five—the "grandest" little house-keeper and a "capital little nurse." Her life is perfectly delightful, full of treats and trips, for Honey Bunch's indulgent Mama and Daddy hung the moon up in the sky just for Honey Bunch. She does everything an ideal child is supposed to do, and she follows all the rules. She knows that green apples make you sick so she doesn't eat them, and therefore she gets the reward of laughing at the little boys who do get sick on them. Her neighbor Norman, who wants to meet an Indian more than anything, is the exemplar of naughtiness, being a boy. Honey Bunch is just the opposite of Norman, who is dead-set on ruining her purified, positively pasteurized world.

Honey Bunch's house has whistling clean linoleum which won't mar or yellow. The only time it ever gets dirty is when Norman tracks mud in. The housekeeper is known as the "laundress." Honey Bunch's whole neigh- . borhood is spruced and brushed and polished—all except Jake Silberman's house.

> "I shouldn't think Mrs. Silberman would like her front
> lawn to look so messy!" sniffed Grace Winters dis-
> approvingly. "My mother would send us out to pick up
> things, if our place looked like this."
> .   *Her First Little Mystery*, pp. 23-24

And Jake Silberman, being Jewish, is frowned upon by these little girls with the perfect names. This reference is only one clue to the prejudices of most of the early children's series books, in which undesirable characters are automatically associated with minority groups. But that's where the mystery is, of course. Mystery always lurks in wild, uncivilized, or foreign landscapes that threaten to spill over. Solving a mystery is like tidying. You can't have a perfectly laundered neighborhood as long as uncouth strangers are hanging about! The large, well-appointed suburban house with waxed floors, a contented pussy cat, a dainty embroidered handkerchief of a yard and a groomed Mommy and Daddy—that's the berries! At the end of her big airplane adventure Honey Bunch says happily, "Let's hurry home . . . I'd rather live home than anywhere else in the world." (*Her First Trip in an Airplane*, p. 187)

Honey Bunch is so conditioned to homey comforts that when she travels she packs very wisely.

> "I can't stop to pet you now, Lady Clare," said the little girl. "I have too much work to do."
>
> With Hilda and the other dolls watching, she began sorting doll garments. It was hard to decide just what to pack. Hilda could wear her traveling clothes, but she would need many changes for the days at the Big Fair.
>
> Honey Bunch chose sensible gingham frocks which would wash easily. She also packed two party dresses, a silk cloak, and a bathing suit. Hats took up more room than anything else.
>
> *Her First Trip to a Big Fair*, p. 56

Honey Bunch proudly plunges into her doll's washing. "She had her own soap chips, tiny wringer and line with small clothespins."

> Honey Bunch knew exactly how to do a washing for she had watched the laundress many times. First she poured soap chips into the bottom of the basin. Then she turned warm water over them. Hot water would be much better, thought Honey Bunch, but her mother never allowed her to use it for fear she might burn herself.
>
> The soap chips did not melt very well. The little girl

stirred and stirred until at last they were all gone and the water was full of bubbles.

Her First Trip to a Big Fair, pp. 62-63

It is ironic that Mrs. Miller, not Honey Bunch's mother, is the laundress (her mother is freed from the necessity of drudgery), while the little girl is trained to be the housekeeper, not trained for freedom and possibility. As with trips, the books hold up one image of life and teach another.

Honey Bunch has a tomboy sidekick, a little cousin named Stub who is built like a football and is always stubbing her toe and tearing her dress. Stub can't do anything right. She is bound and determined not to be conventional. When Honey Bunch's friend Ida talks about marriage, Stub resists.

> "It must be fun to get married and have people send you things."
>
> "I'd like a tool-chest," Stub declared. "Would anyone send me a tool-chest if I got married?"
>
> "That isn't a lady-present," objected Grace Winters. "I never heard of anyone getting a tool-chest for a wedding present."
>
> Stub said if she could not have a tool-chest she would not get married, and Honey Bunch said she thought a tea set was much nicer than a tool-chest.
>
> "A tea set!" Stub remarked in scorn. "Ho, anybody can have a tea set. Why, I wouldn't care if I never had a tea set."
>
> *Her First Little Mystery*, pp. 153-154

Stub gestures so wildly that she crashes a real tea set to the floor.

Stub is the real heroine of that series, as I think I knew even when I first read it, but she isn't meant to be.

I remember the hope chest silverware saleslady who came to our house when I was about fourteen and still not sure if I was going to be a boy or girl (with a name like mine, how could I be sure?). The silverware saleslady wanted me to spend nearly a hundred dollars of my hard-earned berry-picking money on some table tools that I would hide in a box until some hypothetical time that I wasn't sure I wanted to see. I threw a fit and was rude to the woman for trying to box up my hopes in a chest just when I was fixing to flex my wings. Stub was hanging on in my soul.

Honey Bunch is praised while Stub is relentlessly soaped and dressed and disciplined to death. Once when the plane the children are in makes an emergency landing, the passengers walk through a farmer's field for help, but Stub instantly falls into a fresh furrow, and as the farmer picks her up he tells her she looks like a potato.

> "Mother will dust you off with a cloth," he assured the mortified Stub. "Mother always has a damp cloth handy. She can't abide spots."
> Before Stub could object to being called a spot, they had come in sight of the farmhouse.
> *Her First Trip in an Airplane*, p. 170

"Mother" (the farmer's wife, naturally) comes down the path to greet the group, and at the same instant whips a cloth from her apron pocket and gets to work on Stub, pulling her backward and talking all the while about a chicken dinner she just happens to have ready.

Although Stub's rebellion is a forecast of uncertain adolescence—when little girls will read mysteries and imagine themselves as sleuthhounds—the true celebration within these little books is the kitty corner, a motif that recurs in all the girls' series. It is a perfect world in miniature, a little elf nook, a playhouse, a gingerbread cottage, an English garden in a terrarium, a hideaway in an attic. Honey Bunch is ecstatic when she sees the houses of Red Riding Hood and the Three Bears in a pre-Disneyland garden in California. Make-believe Brownies peer through the bushes. The scene is just like her storybook. At the Big Fair, Honey Bunch and Stub visit a fairyland and eat ice cream in a child-sized restaurant. "The children were happy to see that the dishes of ice cream seemed to be the usual size." (P. 82) At the Big Fair Honey Bunch also visits a Midget Village. "Everything was built to size for them. Beds were short, chairs were small, and most of the furniture would have been just right for Honey Bunch." (P. 115) Honey Bunch is delighted, though she momentarily fears that she will grow up to be a midget.

It's my guess that if she didn't grow up to be a midget, she did help cause some of her readers to become mental and moral midgets, because the books celebrate the protective pussy-nook nestling place, leading children backward toward the womb instead of onward toward adulthood. Before my own Stub alter-ego took over, I was obsessed with a fantasy about a perfect playhouse, an idea I believe I got from Honey Bunch books.

Honey Bunch books celebrate materialist values (the dream of elegant furnishings in a perfect playhouse) as the sources of paradise, for built into the series form is the American dream of infinite possibilities, and in Honey Bunch's luxurious world the thrills of travel, mystery, and novelty are the pleasures of a comfortable superior order. Moreover, in Honey Bunch's day these luxuries were inspiring privileges. Children weren't so jaded as today's jet-weary toddlers, who inherit the sterile outcome of those dreams. Children like Honey Bunch were sometimes forced to be inventive, and the world was smaller and the comforts of wealth rare.

In spite of moments of originality, the main effect of these books was to attune the child to orthodox ways of thinking. Honey Bunch is often clever and amusing, and she makes comical mistakes with words (" 'Is a crisis a time when a bear is after you? ' inquired Honey Bunch gravely. She always liked to learn new words." And Honey Bunch thought traveling on a ship was "shipping."). There are a few glimpses into the way a child thinks.

> That was one thing she meant to do when she was older. She thought it would be great fun to stay awake all night and discover how long a night really was.
> *Her First Trip in an Airplane*, p. 165

But Honey Bunch tries so hard to obey the rules that she often cancels out her own humor, for her cleverness usually has to do with her struggles to perform correctly. ("Honey Bunch was very particular about all her games; she wanted everything to be right." *Her First Trip on the Great Lakes*, p. 3) Honey Bunch is very sensitive to people laughing at her for doing things wrong. I can look back on Honey Bunch with some affection, for if there is a secret mirror somewhere of my early childhood, it is on the pages of *Honey Bunch: Her First Trip to a Big Fair*. I recognize (with both amusement and embarrassment) the way Honey Bunch thinks—puzzling to herself and trying to do what she is supposed to do. She is independent and spirited in her attempts to be obedient. ("No one can change names of lakes after they're printed on maps," declared Honey Bunch.) It takes imagination for her to do the right thing. In Sunday School she learns about the heathen and realizes that some naughty boys who hide their church money to buy lollipops are little heathens, so she decides to rob their cache (just so they would be surprised!) and put it in the collection plate. Honey Bunch is a goody-goody but she is also a little trickster. She sees herself as a perfectly independent and serious person, the way children do see themselves. A child doesn't sentimentalize childhood, or even see the humor in it, the way adults do. On the other hand, of course, the model of obedience is an adult creation. Adults must be truly afraid that children are really savages.

To me the word "honeybunch" is a generic term for books about sweet little girls. Honey Bunch is a term of endearment sometimes used romantically, perhaps sexually. Little girls go through the honeybunch phase, age four to eight. They speak in honeybunch (words of charming obedience), wear honeybunch dresses, smile honeybunch smiles. A honeybunch is a nymphet with a built-in chastity belt. A nymphet is an ideal of seductiveness and a honeybunch is an ideal of pristine domesticity. A nymphet (that dangerous reader of Nancy Drew) is nine to fourteen (declares Humbert Humbert, the expert and connoisseur of Lolitas). During the honeybunch phase there is a calculated adult prevention of the awakening of the nymphet in a little girl. The effort continues until her marriage; from the cradle the girl is oriented backward, to prevent her blossoming and awakening, her growth. The Chinese used to bind their women's feet: we honeybunch our females, our version of constriction. The little girl is cautioned not to expose her crotch: *she* suffers the blame for the salacious thoughts of grown-ups. From infancy she is trained in honeybunch style to be a permanent child. She looks to the future through a rear-view mirror. When she eventually marries, her husband will call her Honey Bunch or Sugar Pie or Little Precious. Honey Bunch Morton (I always think of her as the girl in the rain on the salt) is training to be a housemaid, but she still makes comical errors (called imagination) and isn't big enough to roll dough with an adult rolling pin.

Little girls bred on Honey Bunch soon long to do something exciting—to traipse around with the Bobbsey Twins and Nancy Drew, perhaps, trailing footprints and doing anything in the world but playing house. I suspect the sexism of Honey Bunch, as well as that of elementary school readers, makes sleuthing an exotic alternative. The Princeton study, *Dick and Jane as Victims*, has shown that the elementary textbooks of the sixties (not to mention the frustrated fifties) offered no promise or fulfillment to girls.[1] In the illustrations inside these bland books girls do nothing but watch boys huff and puff. If this is the case, why shouldn't a girl want to follow the spirited adventures of escapist heroines? The next chronological step after a sticky diet of Honey Bunch is the Bobbsey Twins.

3

Bobbsey Bourgeois

I was introduced to the Bobbsey Twins under the Christmas tree at the age of eight. It is my impression that I went straight to my favorite chair with a sack of hard candies and didn't get up for three years, after reading all forty of the series at least a dozen times each. By age ten or eleven, I was desperate. How come the Bobbseys got to do not just one or two thrilling things—like the kid in class who went to the State Fair—but *all* the thrilling things? Thrills seemed to be only in books, yet these stories seemed so real, not like far-fetched fairy tales about giants and dragons. Why not just one little journey to Windmill Cottage or Indian Hollow? Or one simple little jewel robbery to solve?

The Bobbseys were my idols and my parents took advantage of my adoration. The Bobbsey Twins don't leave their clothes on the floor! The Bobbsey Twins wash behind *their* ears! The Bobbsey Twins speak when spoken to. At their school it was against the rules to speak aloud during school hours; at my school there was no such thing as a class discussion. You listen, and obey, and wonders will never cease. The Bobbsey Twins even had angels watching over them. I thought I did too.

The Bobbseys have been almost as busy as "Laura Lee Hope," the lovely pseudonym who has written a new Bobbsey almost every year for seventy years—sixty-six titles, some revised half a dozen times! The world is saturated with Bobbseys, nearly sixty million of them. Russel Nye in *The Unembarrassed Muse*, a history of popular culture, says the Bobbsey Twins are "surely the most syrupy girls' books ever written,"[1] but I disagree. Stratemeyer books supplant sentiment with action. The characters are morally upright and the books end happily, but sloppy emotions and meaningful moralities are shunned in favor of zestful pursuits. The characterizations are so slim and the language so sparse it is hard to say that they are ever drippy. Sentiment implies pause for indulgence and Stratemeyer's characters hardly ever pause for a minute, except to eat. Not only that, but the Bobbsey Twins—an ideal package of two sets of boy-girl twins—are archetypal: they stroke the deepest longings of a child for a soulmate. The double theme is recurrent in children's literature, and the Bobbseys, more than others, have capitalized on this desire children have for a mirror-image that talks, sure proof that one has an identity. Reading the Bobbsey Twins, a little girl—anywhere from six to twelve—can imagine a union with someone just like herself, but of the opposite sex. One set of twins is fair and the other dark, but the books never stress any other individual differences, except for sex. Each set of twins is simply twins, and that means they are *exactly* alike. But as we shall see, the sexual distinction makes a world of difference.

Another reason for the initial popularity of the Bobbseys, who started their career in 1904, was their affluence. They lived in a comfortable three-story house with faithful servants, running water, a piano, and a full pantry with a flour barrel. They made a big to-do over Christmas and rode in a handsome carriage and had perfectly splendid times. Dark-haired Nan and Bert were eight, and light, fluffy Flossie and Freddie, who could barely talk, were four. After the series got underway and ran out of baby talk and childish charms, Nan and Bert advanced to twelve and Flossie and Freddie got stuck at age six.

The old-fashioned world of the first two decades of the Bobbseys is small and secure, and a fifty-mile drive in a horseless carriage is an incredible journey with a picnic and several incidents along the way. The children invent their own games and make things—a pasteboard village of shoe boxes, an igloo in the snow with a bay window, a bob sled, an ice boat, and snowshoes. They go for a spectacular outing in a sleigh. They make whoopee in the snow all day long, for they live where there are several snow storms even before Thanksgiving. It's as snowy as the Arctic in Lakeport, but there are even greater pleasures on their exotic northern journeys to such places as "Snow Lodge" and "Cedar Camp" and "Eskimo Land."

Snow Lodge! *The Bobbsey Twins at Snow Lodge* is a major source of all my secret dreams of a cozy nest.

> How warm and cozy it was in Snow Lodge! How bright were the lights, and how the big fire blazed, crackled and roared up the chimney! And what a delightful smell came from the kitchen!
>
> *The Bobbsey Twins at Snow Lodge*, p. 147

The books themselves are fictional nests, escapes from the cruel real landscape. The Bobbseys live in a perfect Christmas-card world, and their readers can never consume enough of their superior pleasures. Though they live in the cold, cold North, that is nothing. No little twin ever gets cold or wears thin mittens. They had all that splendid snow, while I lived in the dull, hot ordinary South where snow became mud after five minutes. The Bobbseys cuddle cozily in a sleigh.

> The big sled with the horses and their jingling bells was soon at the door. Miss Carford had warmed some bricks to put down in the straw, to keep the children's feet warm, and soon, cozily wrapped up, they were on their way home.
> *The Bobbsey Twins at Snow Lodge*, p. 77

Hot bricks in the straw for their feet! In the winter I slept with a hot brick, not because of extreme weather conditions but because we had no furnace. Fireplaces were a tedious necessity, but at centrally heated Snow Lodge fireplaces are a luxury.

> The nights in Snow Lodge were filled with fun. Mr. Bobbsey had bought a barrel of apples, and when the family gathered about the fireplace these were put to roast in the heat of the glowing embers.
> Corn was popped, and then it was eaten, with salt and butter on, or with melted sugar poured over it. Sometimes they would make candy.
> *The Bobbsey Twins at Snow Lodge*, p. 159

This is how it is supposed to be! Getting lost in a Bobbsey book is just like snuggling into a teapot cozy. These rare comforts tease the less fortunate readers. Even when the older twins get lost in the woods during a blizzard, they cleverly construct a little haven by piling branches around three trees and letting the snow cover them. They make hot chocolate from a candy bar and melted snow. And they are so warm that they fall asleep in their little snow tent. That improvised hot chocolate in the snug lean-to has lingered in my mind all these years.

When I began re-reading my Bobbsey books, familiar scenes began leaping to life across twenty years, memories that might otherwise have been forever buried. In *The Bobbsey Twins at Cedar Camp* I read about the twins sliding down a smooth and slippery pine-needled slope. Those fragrant pine needles came rushing back to me in a dazzling whirl of images, and I realized that I have carried that sense-memory with me every time I have been in the woods. My imaginative experience has been intermeshed with my physical experience so that I know what it is like to slide on pine needles, though I have never done it.

The Bobbseys, I decided, were also the source of many of my ideas, prejudices, and expectations. They were like cookie cutters on my imagination. A perfect family, they had delicately delineated roles as carefully balanced as the branches of a hanging mobile. The family needs little description because it is composed of such familiar stereotypes (and there never is any description). Daddy Bobbsey, boss-man, is protector and provider and Santa Claus. Mrs. Bobbsey, whose first name is almost forgotten (she calls her husband "Dick"; he calls her "Mrs. Bobbsey"), has no personal identity. She is simply there, invisibly reliable, like walls and plumbing. She praises and gently reproves the twins. In modern versions her role has expanded: Mr. Bobbsey has receded into the world of business trips, leaving Mrs. Bobbsey to vacation with the children in the station wagon.

The early books contrast the correctness of Nan and Bert with the antics of chubby Flossie and Freddie, who are called "Fat Fairy" and "Fat Fireman" by their adoring daddy. The sex roles are learned early, in spite of Flossie and Freddie's irrepressible mischievousness.

> Freddie was no better than most boys of his age, but he did not forget some of the little polite ways his mamma was continually teaching him. One of these was "ladies first," though Freddie did not always carry it out, especially when he was in a hurry.
>
> *The Bobbsey Twins at School*, p. 10

Flossie, occupied either with her dolls or with pretend games with Freddie, has "a girl's queer way of reasoning." Freddie is impulsive and obsessed with fire trucks. He has a collection of them, including one that squirts. In the first few volumes, the little twins are characterized from an adult perspective as funny and childlike, but conscientious about their proper roles. Once when Flossie makes Freddie hold a doll, he immediately rings his fire bell, throws the doll to Flossie, and rushes off with his engine.

> "That wasn't very nice," pouted Flossie. "Dorothy might have fallen in the snow."
>
> "Can't help it," answered Freddie. "A fireman can't stop for anything."
>
> "But—but—he doesn't have to throw his baby away, does he?" questioned Flossie, with wide open eyes.
>
> "Yes, he does—*ev'rything*."
>
> "But—but supposing he is—is eating his dinner?"
>
> "He has to throw it away, Flossie. Oh, it's awful hard to be a real fireman."
>
> "Would he have to throw his jam away, and his pie?"
>
> "Yes."
>
> "Then I wouldn't be a fireman, not for a—a houseful of gold!" said Flossie, and marched back into the house with her doll.
>
> *The Bobbsey Twins*, p. 67

And in kindergarten at age five, a new world opens up for Flossie and Freddie.

> "We'll soon be reading books," boasted Freddie, on his way home one day. "And I'm going to read all about firemen, soldiers, and Indians."
> "Oh, I'm not," said Flossie. "I'm going to read how to be a nurse, so I can take care of you when you're hurt."
>
> *The Bobbsey Twins at School*, p. 165

So there you are.

The books create an illusion that adventure is the process of learning the roles, although the roles of Mamma and Daddy Bobbsey are dull. Nan is "quite a little housekeeper" and nursemaid to Flossie and Freddie. "She seemed like a little mother to them at times, though she was only four years older." (*The Bobbsey Twins at School*, p. 72) Nan, like Bert, is tops at anything she tries, which isn't much. She wins a peanut race easily and is interested in "patches and tidies" and making jumble chocolates. The reader, at least, is able to lose herself in the excitement of the book, but what is Nan doing? Although she is given more attention in later books, the vacuum of a ten-year-old girl's life can be illustrated in *The Bobbsey Twins in the Great City*, which consists almost entirely of episodes in which the smaller twins "gets losted." Freddie falls into an aquarium and has a fine ride on a turtle. Flossie runs into an elephant's cage to rescue her apple and gives everyone a heart attack. They get lost on the subway and are forever running away after fancies of the moment. Bert gets to do some clever things, like build an ice-boat, but Nan Bobbsey does nothing whatever in the whole Great City of New York except buy a workbasket. Nan is ten, when a little girl is too old for dolls and pranks, too young for boys and barred from their games, halfway between Honey Bunch and nymphet. Bert is going to paddle his own canoe somewhere, and Nan is wistful.

> "Wouldn't you let me paddle with you?" asked Nan. "I know how—a little."
>> *The Bobbsey Twins in the Great City*, p. 167

Nan's alienation is probably not noticeable to the child, because adventure is going on and Nan tags along, wagging her finger at Freddie and appearing to enjoy herself. She has a firm role—as mini-parent, non-child, serious-minded little woman.

Bert Bobbsey acts out his manhood by winning contests and beating the town bully, Danny Rugg, whose aim in life is to play mean tricks on the Bobbseys. Danny Rugg is such a pest that Bert is not above cutting a tree down to get Danny out of it. Mr. Bobbsey is relieved his son isn't a coward and Mrs. Bobbsey cries but bathes Bert's cut lip proudly. Danny Rugg is severely punished for his misdeeds, but when the Bobbsey Twins do wrong they have to stay in the house for an hour instead of playing outdoors. This rarely happens, but when it does the twins fill up on wisdom like thirsty plants, while Danny Rugg never learns a thing. It is a rule in juvenile series fiction that sleuths never misbehave. Naughty children can't follow clues any better than they can follow rules.

In the newer Bobbsey books, Danny causes trouble at the twins' vacation spots, anywhere from Canada to Africa. It usually happens that Mrs. Bobbsey is in the grocery store and runs into Mrs. Rugg and chats awhile and finds out that the Ruggs are going to the exact same place as the Bobbseys, and so Danny shows up, to the twins' dismay, and wreaks haywire and havoc. The device is a regular favorite.

Danny is an obligatory bully whose dirty doings function to glorify the unified strength of the Bobbsey family, in the same way the antics of Stub and Norman reinforce Honey Bunch's sweetness. The Bobbseys, like Honey Bunch's family, are exemplars of the nuclear family—our authorities, our models. Bobbseys are winners. Not everyone can be a Bobbsey. In team sports, Bert is always on the winning side. Nan usually wins girls' games but never competes with boys. It isn't so important for girls to win in Bobbseyland, and Nan never forgets that her brother is her superior.

The winners' values are inherited from Horatio Alger books, which influenced the Stratemeyer creations considerably. Alger heroes struggled against mountainous barriers to win material rewards and prestige. The Bobbseys take up where the Alger books leave off, and so a curious thing happens. Winning loses its context and becomes a fundamental assumption behind an American me-first mentality. In Alger books, the winners were rewarded for their strivings; in the Bobbsey books rewards are plentiful, but the struggles are minor, and so there is a shift in emphasis—to winning for the sake of winning. It is a double standard in which the heroes make much ado about nothing, for there are no obstacles greater than a bully's taunts or the awkward mishaps of daily life. As a result, the books celebrate and perpetuate some outdated values which turn into stereotypes of good and evil. The sources of good are the property owners and businessmen, the "haves" and "winners," the people who run the world. The proper division of authority is male power and female domesticity. The sources of evil are (1) people too cheap to work for a living, and (2) just plain meanness. There is an accounting for some poor people who reveal nobility of purpose—meaning that they submit to the authorities but have been waylaid by the evil forces. The way you recognize the fallen poor is that even though they live in a run-down section of town their houses are clean and their lawns are neatly trimmed and their flowers are blooming. They wear clean, but faded, garments. Otherwise, poverty is a sure source of evil: this was so throughout the clean, well-lighted children's series books until the late 1950s.

Models of authority are insisted upon in the Bobbsey Twins series, not only through obvious sexism but through red-white-and-blue patriotism and through extensive racism. The Bobbsey Twins celebrate the Fourth of July several times without aging. They join patriotic parades, solve their own *Red, White and Blue Mystery* (in 1971), and know the flag rules by heart. America is wonderful. When they travel to the land of cotton in 1942 they pass through "historic country" and stop to read the tablets on houses and in parks. "These told of some stirring action during the Civil War, or showed where some brave soldier had lost his life."

> "Golly, I never knew we had so many heroes," said Freddie after one of these stops. "America's a fine country to live in, isn't it, Daddy?"
>
> "Yes, indeed, and don't you ever forget it," said Mr. Bobbsey heartily.
>
> *The Bobbsey Twins in the Land of Cotton*, p. 122

Presently the Bobbseys roll up to the cotton plantation they are visiting. Across the road are the cabins (left over from slave days) of the workers. "Aren't they cute!" exclaims Flossie. The twins go out to the fields with the "pickaninnies" and pick cotton for a morning. The plantation owner offers a prize to the one who picks the most and Bert wins. The cotton pickers dress gaily and sing a lot.

"They must like their work," said Nan. "They seem so happy."

"Cotton picking is healthful exercise," smiled the plantation owner.

He said no more, but the children knew the workers were happy because they liked Colonel Percy.

The Bobbsey Twins in the Land of Cotton, p. 134

The quote demonstrates perfectly and blatantly the insidious chauvinism of the books—stories which exalt a belief that black people love their work because their boss is kind, stories which rationalize away the moral question of racism with the excuse that back-breaking labor is excellent exercise! With such propagandistic content, these books are downright dangerous. And so alluring, with their placid, delightful surface! The racist assumptions are basic to most of the series books I read as a child, but the series stories were merely a barometer of society, rather than deliberate propaganda. Most of our popular culture tends to mirror and reinforce standard values, and what is worse than the Bobbsey Twins is the injustice of the society they reflect.

But the Bobbseys are at the top. They can afford generosity, especially to their servants, portrayed as shuffle-footed black lackeys.

Mr. Bobbsey was a prosperous lumber merchant. Other members of the household were Dinah and Sam Johnson. Dinah was the cook, fat and good-natured. Sam was her husband, slim and also good-natured. He did all sorts of work about the place, from making garden to shoveling snow.

The Bobbsey Twins at Snow Lodge, p. 17

Well, it's reassuring to know that good-natured Sam and Dinah aren't still pissed off about slavery. The Bobbsey

"OH, MAH GOODNESS! WHO DONE LEFT IT YEAH?"
The Bobbsey Twins and Baby May   Frontispiece (Page 33)

The Bobbsey Twins series promoted stereotyped characters, including an Aunt Jemima portrayal of Dinah the cook as illustrated. Later books omitted racial stereotypes.

books try to take the edge off injustice by making it natural, sweet, quaint, or loving: that is, they make the obvious blind cultural assumptions about white supremacy, translated as "They like to live that way." The Bobbseys include the servants in the family, sometimes helping Dinah set the table or taking her on their vacations. At Christmas they buy "useful presents for the cook—large aprons, warm shoes, an umbrella, and a bright shawl that Dinah had been wanting for a long time." (*The Bobbsey Twins at Snow Lodge*, p. 97) Dinah is portrayed as Aunt Jemima, kerchief and all. The servants' position in the family is understood clearly by the smaller twins. Among Flossie's dolls (including the 1910 version of Barbie and all her wardrobes) are two cripples and a black boy.

> ... Jujube, a colored boy, dressed in a fiery suit of red, with a blue cap and real rubber boots. This doll had been from Sam and Dinah and had been much admired at first, but now taken out only when all the others went too.
>
> "He doesn't really belong to the family, you know," Flossie would explain to her friends. "But I have to keep him, for mamma says there is no colored orphan asylum for dolls. Besides, I don't think Sam and Dinah would like to see their doll child in an asylum." The dolls were all kept in a row in a big bureau drawer at the top of the house, but Flossie always took pains to separate Jujube from the rest by placing the cover of a pasteboard box between them.
>
> *The Bobbsey Twins*, p. 68

In the late 1950s Stratemeyer Syndicate began to excise the overt racism from the Bobbsey Twins and other series, but it could not remove the fundamental assumptions without abandoning the Bobbseys and starting over again. The dialect was changed to white English, but the servants' roles did not change. To avoid the problem, the writers finally left out Dinah and Sam altogether.

Indians are treated as if they are either wooden Indians or Hollywood Indians, and Gypsies have fared no better with the Bobbseys, since Gypsies violate everything a Bobbsey stands for.[2] The blacks at least seem to know their place, but you can never tell about a Gypsy. The Bobbseys go to Blueberry Island for a friendly family vacation and are plagued to death by sneaky Gypsies who steal their dog and cat. A local boy tells them:

> "They're a shiftless lot. They don't work and they take what don't belong to 'em. They're too lazy to hunt with a gun, so they snare birds in a net. Why, they'll even eat sparrows."
>
> *The Bobbsey Twins on Blueberry Island*, p. 206

The Bobbseys go out with their shiny new pails to pick blueberries and those confounded Gypsies have picked them all! Nan is scared to death, "looking over her shoulder into the bushes, as though she feared a dark-faced man, with gold rings in his ears, might step out any moment and make a grab for Flossie or Freddie." (P. 133)

> "Gypsies on the island, eh?" remarked Mr. Bobbsey. "Well, I suppose they think they have a right to camp here. But I'll see about it. Maybe some of them are all right, but I don't like the idea of staying here if the place is going to be overrun with them. I must see about it."
>
> *The Bobbsey Twins on Blueberry Island*, p. 135

The Bobbsey Twins think they are free to pick blueberries or cotton, whatever they want, for picking blueberries is a free pleasure, hardly linked with survival—of which the privileged are not aware. They are the first flower children of the century.

In the world of the Bobbsey Twins, the city and the country are not contradictory places. The Bobbseys love the country—it's as grand as the zoo or Disneyland or Christmas. They visit perfect farms nestled in valleys with red barns and trout streams and gentle barnyard creatures. They visit the paradises of Clover Bank, Cherry Corners, and Meadow Brook. Wonderful "plain folks" offer them fresh milk and butter and homemade peach cobblers. As late as the 1940s, when the Bobbseys motored in the family car, obliging farmers provided them with bed and breakfast and picnic luncheons in wicker hampers. This is what the well-to-do town people—people who had "made it"—expected, apparently, in the days before motels. In one book, the twins make friends with an old woodchopper who lives in a remote log cabin. Then they go to New York and visit a department store with a camping display—"a sort of woodland scene." It has real moss and dirt, a spring, a real tent and cots and two real woodsmen doing their thing in the display window, all to advertise camping goods.

> "It certainly looks like the real thing," was Bert's remark. "And the best part of it is, everything is so new and clean."
>
> *The Bobbsey Twins in a Great City*, p. 166

The department-store owner turns out to be the long-lost brother of the old woodsman and the Bobbsey Twins reunite the pair. The woodchopper gets to move to the Great City to live the real life with the department-store owner and he doesn't have to chop wood any more.

The Bobbsey series spans a range of possible fantasies of deliverance, so that the hardship one is being delivered from is completely forgotten. In a world of unlimited opportunity, what is the challenge for the winner? What are the obstacles? All the world's a vacation, and nothing much more fulfilling than tourism can finally result. The Bobbseys visit all the typical tourist places—the mountains, the seashore, the country, the West, carnivals, cities, lakes, islands, woods. Each is just like it is supposed to be.

So when I read the Bobbseys I was filled with longing. Between the ages of nine and eleven I was in a tizzy over *The Bobbsey Twins in Mexico*. I wanted to go to Mexico so badly I can still taste the tacos. This is the way I remember it. The Bobbsey Twins met Mateo and Maria from Mexico. Their father was a chocolate king and they were visiting Lakeport on business. Mr. Bobbsey decided to take his brood to Mexico to see about buying some trees for his lumberyard. Nan learned Spanish and they had a farewell party with a Mexican piñata and party favors. So many things happened before they left that they didn't get to Mexico until Chapter 17. Nan lost her friends' chihuahua and got stuck on top of a ferris wheel, and Flossie and Freddie performed in a circus as substitute midgets. In Mexico Bert got blown off an Aztec pyramid by a furious wind, they visited a chocolate factory, saw chewing gum trees at their friends' endless hacienda, and went boating on a floating garden in a boat named the *Lolita*. Strangest of all, they met some elves in the Mexican forest, who agreed to take Flossie and Freddie's circus job. And then the twins brought back souvenirs for all their friends.

The Bobbsey's "authentic" adventures reduced starved readers to souvenir hunters. Even for a child less isolated than I was, there is still a strong appeal of authority—authorized fun, goals, behavior. Souvenirs are important clues to the reality of authority. The Washington Monument is a clue to the country—a symbol, like the flag which the Bobbseys flap wildly, of the authority of government. The nation's Capitol, gleaming against a blue sky, is another clue, and you can buy a plastic miniature to prove it to the folks back home. Snapshots, like coded messages, footprints and fingerprints, are clues.

The Bobbsey hierarchical world view is paradoxically a slave mentality, flagrantly Christian and American. In order to be free, you must worship. In order to be a winner, you must serve higher authorities, and winning means ascending the scale so that others are your slaves: step on others to get to the top, be a status seeker. It's the Great Chain of Being, and just as medieval:

> God
> Angels
> Bobbseys
> Workers
> Slaves
> Animals
> Vegetables
> Rocks
> Etc.

The Great Chain of Bobbsey offers no personal identity (no sacredness of inner resources) but that of a fan snatching at God's coattails. If the goal is the big time, then there is no earthly way to get there except through the process of consuming. The American dream is the desire to absorb, know, and conquer everything, to go everywhere and to do it all, and to take whatever is free, even if you can't use it. We even have eating contests to show off our gluttony.

I have recurring food dreams where I stand in a cafeteria line and have to choose from a thousand beautiful foods and by the time I get done choosing it's time to wake up and I don't get to eat the food. I've had these dreams my whole life, starting about the time I met the Bobbsey Twins. It is the principle of having eyes bigger than your stomach, wanting more than you can have, daring indigestion. America, when it was discovered by the Europeans, appeared to be a consumer's paradise. The settlers came over here and saw this whole banquet of a beautiful land and their eyes were bigger than their stomachs and so they chopped down more than they could use and called it the United States. Mr. Bobbsey is a lumber merchant and his twins are the children of a forest rapist!

In newer books the twins eat cookies in every chapter and stop at every refreshment stand in sight. They drink a lot of soda pop and when they sit down to a meal the reader is given the full menu. If the reader is satiated with every other pleasure, at least she will be hungry three times a day. In the modern books, the Bobbseys are less innocent, their material appurtenances more taken for granted as their privileges have become more commonplace. They have begun vigorously to protect the values of their upper-class world and so have set about solving mysteries. The Bobbseys are now known as amateur detectives and there is a purpose to childhood after all. (Even the Honey Bunch books were turned into a mystery series in the 1950s.) There used to be a lot of simple fun in the childlike defense of innocence, but nowadays the twins are super-serious. They must defend that station-wagon scene like crazy.

Flossie and Freddie no longer play pretend games. They report clues to the older twins. It's awful hard being a Bobbsey sleuth.

The plot pattern of the revised books is well illustrated by the blurb of *The Red, White and Blue Mystery*.[3]

"I hope I never meet the monster!" says Flossie Bobbsey as weird howls come from a crack in a hillside on the farm of the twins' friends in Virginia. The young detectives not only meet the howler, but catch a thief and discover a special treasure—one of our nation's very first flags. It had been hidden during the Revolution by the young girl who made it. What fun the Bobbseys have in this All-American adventure! They not only solve the mysteries but learn about the early days of our country by visiting the quaint shops and streets of Colonial Williamsburg.

All the newer Bobbsey books are essentially the same story: a monster or ghost which the twins prove to be maliciously human; a crook chase; a treasure; and a trip to a fascinating place. It is interesting that a major focus is on destroying the supernatural—that ultimate threat of the unknown. It is still a snug Bobbsey world (though it isn't so cold now in Lakeport, which seems to have shifted south) when justice is done.

The Bobbsey Twins books build up a dream version of life, in the guise of the castle just around the corner, and prepare the little armchair sleuth for the more serious and desperate dreams of adolescence. The Bobbsey fan is like an addict, lustily absorbing each new story to assuage a confused longing, only to have it deepened. Exhausted by her darlings' exploits, she will have no choice but to graduate to Nancy Drew and start pursuing mysteries in earnest.

4

Nancy Drew: The Once and Future Prom Queen

On the secret shelf in my study stand all my girlhood books: the green Bobbsey books with Pennsylvania Dutch hexes on their covers; the brown Hardy Boys (I did have a few); the blue-gray Beverly Grays and Vicki Barrs; the red Judy Boltons and Cherry Ameses; and the most impressive looking of them all, the royal blue Nancy Drews.

It occurs to me now that Nancy's color *is* blue, and that this may be an important tip-off to the mystery of the girl in blue. Blue, after all, is our culture's chromatic emblem of boyhood. Blue is the color of baby boy bunting, of toy airplanes and motorcycles, of the vast skies and seas that Tom Swift and the Hardy Boys and all their rambunctious cohorts busily conquer. And blue is also a classy expression of reserved, WASPish "good taste." It's a perfect complement to Nancy's blond hair. And it's patriotic. Not only are the books blue, but Nancy's eyes are blue, and her sporty roadster is blue as well. In fact, my abiding image of Nancy is of her in a blue suit serenely driving her very own blue auto.

Nancy wears her blue primly, of course, and the reader of a Nancy book is never allowed to forget that our heroine—gunning down the highway after a gang of crooks—is a sweet young lady who dresses nicely and enjoys having tea with little cakes. But, as if authorized by a blue uniform, she is more boyishly daring than your average female adventurer. Nancy manages the almost impossible feat of being wholesomely "feminine"—glamorous, gracious, stylish, tactful—while also proving herself strong, resourceful, and bold, the most independent of the girl sleuths. Nancy is a paradox, and she is also the most popular girl detective in the world.

There had been nothing in children's books like the success of Nancy Drew. She solved her first mystery in 1929, serenely ignoring the world crashing all around. By 1933 Macy's in New York was selling 6,000 Nancy Drews (ten titles by then) at Christmas, compared with 3,750 of Bomba, the Jungle Boy, the most popular boys' series.[1] Edward Stratemeyer wrote (or plotted) the first three Nancy mysteries under the name "Carolyn Keene," but he did not live to see the spectacular rise of the new type of heroine he had helped fashion. His daughter, Harriet S. Adams, took over the series, pseudonym and all, and has written a volume nearly every year since 1930. She estimates that sixty million copies of Nancy Drew books have been sold. Nancy has managed to solve more than fifty mysteries (plus two or three versions of those which have been updated from time to time), most of them in the summer of her eighteenth year.

Much of Nancy's popularity, like that of the Bobbseys, comes from the appeal of her high-class advantages. She has everything a girl could want—a mere given for the privilege of sleuthing, Nancy-style. She lives, with her understanding and trusting Dad, in a comfortable, tree-shaded Colonial brick home with a circular drive—the affluent American version of fairyland. Her lovely home is located in elusive River Heights, a city which is variously Eastern and Mid-Western. Nancy has an endless wardrobe (with numerous "sports dresses," whatever those are), a dependable and worshipful boyfriend, and her own car. She gets to go anywhere in the world she wishes and she doesn't have to go to school. And for all her privileges, she is utterly unspoiled and charming. She is independent, brilliant, poised, courageous, kind, attractive, gracious, well-to-do—i.e., free, white, and sixteen.

Nancy is sixteen at the beginning of the series, then advances to eighteen, but she always behaves as if she is about thirty. She hasn't a shred of childishness in her. She is as immaculate and self-possessed as a Miss America on tour. She is as cool as Mata Hari and as sweet as Betty Crocker. She plays parent to frightened children and victims of misfortune, allaying fears and inspiring rapturous confidence instantly with her soothing, reasonable voice. The reason given for her astonishing self-possession is that her experience has matured her:

> Since the death of her mother many years before, Nancy had managed the household. On the whole she had engineered everything so skillfully that her father little dreamed of the heavy responsibility which rested upon her shoulders.
>
> *The Mystery at Lilac Inn*, p. 12

In short, there's no nagging mamma around to needle Nancy. Most other sleuths have mothers, but the degree to which the mothers interfere is the measure of how much fun the sleuth is allowed to have. The Hardy Boys have a mother, but she is hidden so successfully that the reader never suspects she has any power. Nancy has a housekeeper, Mrs. Hannah Gruen, a jackie-of-all-chores who plays the maternal role (worry-wart and cook), but Nancy is mistress of the household, and her power extends beyond the home. She gets instant service from policemen, even in a strange town. She calls up, identifies herself and says,

> "Please send a plainclothes detective at once. I'll meet him in the lobby here and explain everything to him when he arrives. How will I know him?"
> "He'll pretend to be lame."
>
> *The Clue in the Crumbling Wall*, p. 123

No questions asked.

Nancy is the type of person who leaves calling cards, another indication of her maturity and authority. She doesn't have to resort to any humiliating wheedling, whims, or fits, like most kids, to get what she wants. She doesn't have to beg to go on an impossible trip to Florida, as I once did. When she needs to follow up a clue, she says simply (but cunningly), "Dad, do you suppose you could manage a Florida vacation next week?" (*The Clue of the Black Keys*, p. 126) Obliging Dad lets her make the trip without him. And, once there, Nancy finds it necessary to pursue the mystery to Mexico, a trip she makes with ease. (I still haven't been to Florida, and I've abandoned all hope of ever seeing Mexico.)

Readers respect Nancy's seriousness. She is usually too busy solving a mystery to engage in frivolity. Only in rare instances does she lose her cool, and then only momentarily. Even when she is locked in a room full of spiders, she doesn't get the creeps, as any real girl would. Instead, she proceeds logically, calmly, to find an exit. At all times Nancy possesses infinite courage, calm, and modesty:

The Girl Sleuth 51

Bess was concerned. "Why, Nancy, you might have slipped off that roof and been killed!"

Nancy grinned. "I guess I'm just a tough old sleuth," she answered.

The Clue of the Broken Locket (rev. ed.), p. 74

"As for Nancy and her exploits, girls have thrilled vicariously to their heroine's unusual ability. How all of us, in our childhood, aspired to the heroic!" comments Andrew E. Svenson of Stratemeyer Syndicate. Nancy's abilities certainly left me limp with longing. I couldn't even answer roll call in the schoolroom without blushing, so my adulation of Nancy was understandable. I wonder how many little girls—especially shy ones—secretly imagine themselves as circus performers or movie stars. I did, certainly. Nancy acts out those fantasies. She is a bareback ballerina in a circus, a dancer, an actress. When a leading lady is taken ill, Nancy replaces her after rehearsing only once. (Once! I feel as if I have rehearsed my whole life.) Even when she has to fall back on purely feminine arts, she is applauded: her flowers win first prize in the flower show. Nancy is so accomplished that she can lie bound and gagged in a dank basement or snowed-in cabin for as much as twenty-four hours without freezing to death or wetting her pants. And she is knowledgeable about any convenient subject. She always has, at tongue's tip, virtually any information needed on a case. She once did an overnight cram course in archaeology and passed a college test with a brilliant score. The ease of her achievements is inspiring to every bandy-legged or pimply little girl who follows her adventures. In one book Nancy discovers an injured man who has a shell fragment in his forehead. When the doctor arrives, her friends respectfully leave. "Nancy alone remained to assist the man of medicine."

"Have you a steady nerve?" he questioned her.

"I think so," Nancy answered quietly.

The operation was not a pleasant thing to witness, but at last it was finished, and the doctor declared that the patient had an excellent chance to recover.

"Have you ever studied nursing?" he asked Nancy abruptly.

"Oh, no, I've had only training in first aid."

"You seem to have missed your calling," the doctor told her with a smile. "You appear to have a natural bent for nursing."

Nancy flushed at the praise.

The Haunted Bridge, p. 121

If girls cannot aspire to important careers in medicine and law and business, they can be rewarded for assisting men, and Nancy dares the limits of the female nurse-maid-secretary role. Her father, a lawyer, admires her talents so much that he makes her his special assistant, and she frequently shows him up.

Not only is Nancy perfect, but she possesses the ideal qualities of each age and sex: child, girl, teenager, boy, and adult. She has made a daring stride into adulthood, and she also trespasses into male territory without giving up female advantages. Nancy's adolescent readers may not know whether to shave their legs and giggle to attract the boys they are discovering, or to join the boys' games and emulate them to win their approval, but Nancy does both; although, being pure, she gives no thought at all to romance—or, flush, sex.

Nancy's two sidekicks, squeamish Bess and tomboy George, emphasize this ambivalence. Bess Marvin is "dainty" and "feminine," and George Fayne, her cousin, is boyish and says "Hypers" a lot. George wears her hair short and scoffs at Bess's romantic ideas.

"SHE IS THE THIEF!" THE MAN CRIED TRIUMPHANTLY.
The Clue of the Broken Locket

Pictures of Nancy Drew and her two sidekicks illustrate the series' stereotypical separation of female qualities into distinct extremes. Squeamish Bess and tomboy George accompany Nancy (in the driver's seat), the daring ideal whose independence threatens villains.

"Old lace is valuable," declared Bess. . . . "Oh," she sighed, "we girls should wear more lace. In olden times ladies appreciated its lure! The great ladies of the Court knew its power!"

"Yes," said George with a grimace. "You know who first thought of lace, don't you? Fishermen. The first lace was a fish net, made to lure food from the sea!"

"George, you're disgustingly unromantic," said her cousin.

The Secret in the Old Attic, p. 136

When Nancy and her friends tour Pleasant Hedges, a run-down estate where Nancy is working on a case, they inspect the old slave quarters.

"What a story this place could tell," sighed Bess. "Old mammies crooning, little pickaninnies dancing—"

"You certainly have a good imagination," said George practically. "Without a piece of furniture or a rug or a picture in the place, how can you think of such things?"

The Secret in the Old Attic, p. 17

Bess is the most passive, squeaky-feminine character in girls' mysteries. She is gullible and giggly. She buys a perfume which her friends suspect is a cheap imitation. When a swindler plays on her sympathies, she is sucked into giving money to a nonexistent orphan Indian. In the presence of a handsome male, she flirts self-consciously. ("Bess daintily disciplined her hair with her finger tips." *The Clue of the Black Keys,* p. 20) She is plump because she eats too much, always lapsing into mindless sensuality when fudge sundaes are around. She embodies the stereotype of passive female consumerism. Bess can't keep secrets, or whistle, and most of her thoughts are about boys, fun, and food. She watches the picnic supplies carefully when the girls are traveling, for fear they will starve to death.

Nancy sleuths virtually unaided. George and Bess spend most of their time hanging around, wringing their hands, window shopping or drinking tea, while Nancy figures and figures. They are recognizable only by their loyalty and as mirrors of Nancy's two halves, demonstrating the extreme options open to females—tomboy and fluff-head. The two roles are clumsy, short-sighted examples of the females we are taught to loathe as we become more and more alienated from our selves. When I played at solving mysteries with a girlfriend in 1951, both of us had to contend with all the conflicting impulses to be girls, boys, tomboys, ladies. Nancy serenely pulls all the impulses into one role. George, for all her muscles and ability to climb and row, and her habit of "galloping" into the room, doesn't have the poise and grace which enables Nancy to maneuver slickly through tight situations, and Bess couldn't even begin to try.

The plots of Nancy Drew mysteries are like sonnets—endless variations on an inflexible form. A plot may contain any or all of these elements: the pursuit of at least two separate mysteries which turn out to be astonishingly intertwined; a warning to get off the case; a trip to a quaint or exotic place (with tourist bureau description supplied); the befriending of an innocent victim (a gentle foreign girl, a kindly businessman, a helpless little old lady) who faces ruin if the mystery isn't solved; a romantic story about a tradition or secret in a prominent family; the appearance of twins or doubles; sinister encounters with the villains (burglaries and sabotages, kidnappings and chases); any number of mishaps (including frequent, but not serious, injury to Nancy); and imprisonment of either Nancy or the innocent victim. The ending is usually a crescendo of swift events: catastrophe just as Nancy is about to break the case, rescue by police/friends/family, an easy round-up of the crooks (who can't have gone far in the time it takes for Nancy's loyal protectors to find her), the immediate and crestfallen confession, discovery of the treasure or secret, and celebration and praise of the girl sleuth. Nancy tries to point out that there would have been no victory without the superb aid of her friends, but everyone gives her the credit for solving the mystery.

Nancy Drew plots are based on coincidence. In one book Nancy witnesses a pickpocket performing his art at least a dozen times, and she happens to be snacking at the very hamburger heaven where he is finally arrested. In *The Password to Larkspur Lane*, Nancy happens to be picking larkspurs in her garden when a plane flies over and drops a message which leads her into the mystery. The message, of course, is the password to Larkspur Lane. The workings of mysteries depend on convenient coincidences—mysteries celebrate coincidence. And for readers the longing to solve a mystery is also a desire for a real coincidence. Indeed, it would have been some coincidence if my parents had okayed that trip to Florida. And little girls depend on coincidence. They learn to be passive, and wait for the day when they will coincidentally be in the same room with a handsome man who will coincidentally fall in love with them.

The settings a girl sleuth like Nancy has to work within are all feminine, domestic, aristocratic, slightly Gothic—quaint reminders of a traditional, Victorian, idealized world. They are "enchanting," fascinating and intricate, like enlarged dollhouses. In *The Clue in the Crumbling Wall*, Nancy and her friends explore the grounds of Heath Castle, a replica of an old English castle, which has decayed into a jungle of neglect.

> At the end of the oak-lined avenue the girls came to a weather-stained loggia of stone. Its four handsomely carved pillars rose to support a balcony over which vines trailed. Steps led to the upper part.
>
> Mounting to the balcony, Nancy and her friends obtained a fine view of the near-by gardens. They had been laid out in formal sections, each one bounded by a stone wall or a hedge. Here and there were small circular pools, now heavy with lichens and moss, and fountains with leaf-filled basins.
>
> *The Clue in the Crumbling Wall*, pp. 30-31

They cross a "rustic bridge which spanned a stream so clogged with water lilies that there scarcely was any space between them." A slippery, moss-grown path labeled "Haunted Walk" spooks Bess. They find themselves in "a vine-tangled, fern-matted bower. Two handsome stone vases lay on their sides, cracked from having filled with water which had frozen during the winter." (P. 30) Such rich description is reserved for quaint settings in the Nancy books, for usually the language is formal and sparse. Here, romantic ruin evokes nostalgia for a past order, and it whips up the tidying impulse. A girl sleuth is a kind of gardener for tragic victims. When she enters the case she already envisions the hedges trimmed, the flowers blooming, the grass mowed. The unscrupulous lawyer responsible for the upkeep of Heath Castle has ignored it, as men whose wives are away (in a conventional world) will let the sink pile up with dirty dishes.

The wronged woman in that book, Miss Flower, is also a dedicated gardener, and when her property is recovered she turns the estate into showplace perfection, with a velvety smooth lawn and masses of blooms, before you can say Jack Sprat. The fact that she is crippled and has suffered ten years of woe is irrelevant. The recovery of property rights is like a dose from the fountain of youth.

All mansions in the Nancy books are haunted—not by ghosts but by swindlers seeking secrets. They haunt hidden passages and secret attics in their search for concealed treasure. Scenes about Nancy's discovery of hidden compartments go something like this:

> "I can feel something with my fingers!" Nancy said in an excited voice. "A little bump in the wood!"
>
> "Probably it's a knothole," George contributed skeptically.
>
> "It's a tiny knob!" corrected Nancy. "Girls, I've found a secret compartment!"
>
> *The Secret in the Old Attic*, p. 138

(With hilarious clarity, I see here the girls' mysteries as a celebration of masturbation!) Nancy is called away for five pages and when she returns Bess and George are still tugging at the knob, but as soon as Nancy renews her grip, the panel opens. "Nancy gave the knob a quick jerk sideways. A little door pulled up, revealing a recess below." (P. 143)

Sometimes the mystery revolves around an intricate object which is a miniaturized version of the mansion: a carved brass chest filled with jewelry, an ancient map, a will hidden in an old clock, an ivory charm, an old family album, a broken locket. Two of the most splendid objects appear in *The Clue in the Jewel Box*.

> One piece completely captured the girl's interest. It was a pink enamel Easter egg which stood on a tiny gold pedestal. Its rounded cover was encrusted with delicate gold work. (p. 6)

> Inside, rising from a nest of velvet, was a tiny tree set
> with emeralds. Upon a jeweled branch was perched a
> delicately fashioned nightingale. (p. 30)

This Fabergé-inspired nightingale sings out the clue in
the jewel box—yet another splendid object.

The allure of these objects and settings derives from
the books' essential conservatism. Femininity is safely
enthroned in charming Victorian manses: this is the
tea-party world.

> As the girls sipped their tea and ate delicious, frosted
> cakes, their hostess spoke rather sadly of present daily life
> in her native land so changed from the past.
> *The Clue in the Jewel Box*, pp. 27-28

The most appealing elements of these daredevil girl
sleuth adventure books are (secretly) of this kind: tea
and fancy cakes, romantic settings, food eaten in quaint
places (never a Ho-Jo's), delicious pauses that refresh,
old-fashioned picnics in the woods, precious jewels and
heirlooms. These things are, subtly, more appealing than
the car chases, kidnappings, and burglaries. The word
"dainty" is a subversive affirmation of a feminized
universe. It sneaks in and out of the books like a
delicate gold thread, offsetting the pell-mell action of
the plot. Nancy wears dainty dresses to dainty tea
dances where she nibbles on dainty sandwiches. The
stories seem to satisfy two standards—adventure and
domesticity. But adventure is the superstructure, domesticity the bedrock. The Nancy books give it to the
readers from both sides, and never once betray a
suspicion that they are contradictory. Nancy's daring
exploits release readers from the abyss of sorority teas
and sewing bees while at the same time congratulating
that tea-party and sewing-basket world.

The girl sleuth's quest, then, is not really for the unknown, but for the known, for the familiar. No thugs and smugglers can dwell in their grungy hideouts on canned beans for long when a girl sleuth is around. Solving a mystery, in girls' books, is actually the fictional equivalent of baking a cake, piecing together a quilt or jigsaw puzzle, sewing a fine seam, or spring cleaning.

In her defense of the cozy tea-party scene, Nancy uses traditional feminine wiles, relying on her instincts, intuition, and charm. A sleuth, that is to say, is a sneak. In *The Secret in the Old Attic* Nancy's father assigns her to get information from the secret laboratory of a factory, which may be using a stolen formula. Nancy gets into the factory by cultivating the friendship of the director's daughter, Diane, a conceited girl she dislikes. Nancy arranges to meet Diane "accidentally," and then cajoles the girl into taking her on a tour of the factory. Nancy wears her best party things to arouse Diane's interest and envy. She accomplishes her goal, reaching the secret inner sanctum, where, to divert attention from her real mission, she feigns illness. A workman helps her.

> "Are you sick?" he asked in a coarse, heavy voice.
> Nancy did not want to answer questions. To avoid them she pretended to faint. The act was well timed, for the man, frightened, immediately rushed into the hall for help. The young detective smiled.
>
> *The Secret in the Old Attic*, p. 67

While he is gone, she gleefully snoops, and afterward beguiles a brusque businessman. Her father "could not hide a smile when he heard of her ruse." (P. 69)

Nancy is generally above the low habit of eaves-dropping, but when she "accidentally" overhears something, she always tunes in at the critical moment. No sooner does she hear voices than they say something like "That Drew girl is on our trail!" And Nancy won't snoop around people's private papers without good reason—but there generally is one. Once she is lecturing a young professor on detecting: he hasn't learned to notice things like people's mail and telephone messages. " 'I'm afraid a good detective has to snoop,' Nancy said." (*The Clue of the Black Keys*, p. 92)

To the extent that a girl sleuth is a sneak, some of her wiliest sleuthing involves deceiving her boyfriends or leading them on a merry chase. Nancy won't go out with a creep even if it means missing the dance of the year—until she finds out, of course, that she might pursue some clues there. In *The Haunted Bridge*, Nancy is plagued by the attentions of Mortimer Bartescue, one of the slick, conceited characters Nancy instantly dislikes (her judgment of character is flawless and instantaneous). He is not a criminal, just a "cheap boaster." Nancy, however modest and generous she is, has no room in her heart for people who are uppity and shallow-minded. Mortimer Bartescue is an unpleasant flirt with

> sleek black hair plastered back from an angular, hard face . . . . Obviously he was a braggart, and she rather distrusted his claim that he came from an excellent family.
>
> *The Haunted Bridge*, pp. 6-7

However, she accepts an invitation to a dance because she needs to do some sleuthing.

Although Nancy admires her steady boyfriend, Ned Nickerson, she is not gaga about him and she doesn't treat him much better than she does Mortimer. Ned is a college football star who is as bland as Nancy is blonde and he has nothing on his mind except football and sex. Every time Ned gets Nancy alone a mystery intervenes.

> "Are you willing to help me?" Nancy asked eagerly.
>
> "Of course. I thought you didn't need any assistance."
>
> "Oh, Ned, it was just that I couldn't explain everything, and I'm afraid I can't even now."
>
> "That doesn't matter, Nancy. You tell me what to do and I'll obey orders with no questions asked."
>
> "It may mean ruining your evening, Ned. Are you willing to substitute sleuthing for dancing?"
>
> "We can dance when we get back to River Heights."
>
> "That's the way I feel about it," Nancy agreed in satisfaction. "It may be that I am too hopeful, but I honestly believe matters will come to a climax tonight."
>
> *The Haunted Bridge*, pp. 170-171

Nancy has Ned under her thumb, and she must keep him there if she is to protect her purity. The series is purposely mum about sex, as any girl's premarital life is supposed to be. But as it is in anything that interests adolescents, sex is subtly present. Mysteries are a substitute for sex, since sex is the greatest mystery of all for adolescents. The Nancy Drew books cleverly (and no doubt unintentionally) conceal sexual fascination, especially since Nancy is frequently embarrassed by Ned's attentions. Once Nancy and Ned go to a carnival and get stuck at the top of a ferris wheel. And up there on top of the world Nancy gives way to one of her rare giggles. Pity for Ned that they weren't stuck in the Tunnel of Love.

Ned longs for a moment alone with Nancy, but she diverts his attention toward sleuthing. At the climax of *The Secret of the Golden Pavilion*, Ned unearths the treasure, a long, colored cape of bird feathers.

"Why, this is one of those ceremonial capes made from the extinct o-o bird!" Nancy exclaimed softly. "A museum piece!"

The Secret of the Golden Pavilion, p. 169

Nancy is a scholar, and a scholar is a version of a sleuth, but Ned has only the male's territorial rights in mind. He puts on the cape and struts around proudly like a peacock parading its plumage. Again the mystery intrudes: the thugs come, whisk away Ned's feathers, and imprison the couple in a dungeon. There they are, together at last in the dark, but Nancy urges escape. They find a secret door which won't budge, so Ned throws himself against it.

Ned, down on one knee like a football lineman about to charge his opponents, lunged. His shoulder thudded against the masonry.

"Oh, Ned," Nancy whispered. "You'll break a bone."

The Secret of the Golden Pavilion, p. 172

They escape and Nancy is eager to find their captors and the cape. "This is our chance to do a little sleuthing," she says. Ned reluctantly follows. First, Nancy has to find her shoes and stockings, which she had earlier removed in order to impersonate a white-robed ghost in the moonlight, hoping to frighten the crooks. Poor Ned Nickerson! They could have stayed blissfully in their prison till morning with no questions asked. Nancy had even shed some clothing.

Nancy and her girlfriends are shockingly independent, but a strong moral code guards them. They travel and stay at motels by themselves, and even meet their boyfriends at motels—where they stay in carefully assigned separate rooms. The girls stay only at places with a "charming and homelike atmosphere." A hilarious slip occurs in *The Mystery of the Tolling Bell* when Ned and Nancy have a car accident and have to hitch a ride on a truck to Nancy's boarding-house.

> Then, at Mrs. Chantrey's insistence, Ned accepted an invitation to stay overnight, and everyone wearily went off to his room for a much-needed sleep.
>
> *The Mystery of the Tolling Bell*, p. 154

It is difficult to imagine Ned with everyone sleeping in *his* room! The formal, correct style of the Nancy books tripped over itself in this unconsciously sexist phrase.

Ned and Nancy are "friends" in the early books, and Nancy greets him "cordially" on the phone. Ned strains to win Nancy's approval, but she notices him most when she needs his muscles. On one occasion Ned is eager for their date, while Nancy is preoccupied with her current case.

> "How do you like my new suit?"
> "You look handsome in it," Nancy praised, without noting in detail what he wore.
>
> *The Haunted Bridge*, pp. 168-169

The books affirm a double standard for female sexuality: attention to beauty and clamps on virginity. Nancy has all the glamour of a starlet, but the entrances to her emotions and physical desires are closed up tight. Nancy driving her convertible looks like the come-on car ads, but she resists this passive, seductive image. She is no leisure-lily lolling on tiger upholstery. Her foot is on the accelerator. But indignant male chauvinists are always puncturing her tires or shoving her into a ditch. A girl isn't supposed to drive! She's supposed to be an accessory to a car, like a vinyl steering wheel cozy. Men threaten Nancy because she threatens their masculinity. Crooks and cops alike want to stifle Nancy's energy, but she is smugly superior.

> "I guess those two younger men were pretty annoyed with me!" Nancy thought as she left the police station. "Afraid I'll take some glory from them!"
>
> *The Clue in the Jewel Box*, pp. 147-148

The evil-eyed desperados on Nancy's trail (because she knows too much) are actually insecure old geezers with funny names who draw attention to their basic weaknesses by resorting to clumsy, melodramatic ploys. They use mysterious haunting devices (ghostly bells, phantoms, weird noises) to frighten Nancy away from their hideouts. As soon as Nancy gets a whiff of a mystery, the crooks start hurling rocks through her window, sending crude messages ("Keep off the case or else!"), sabotaging her car, kidnapping right and left—all sorts of ill-tempered tricks. But their underhanded efforts only get Nancy's dander up. She knows instinctively that they are cowards. She keeps her wits and hits them with the weapon they fear most—truth. They can't stand to have such a nosy know-it-all trip them up. In fact, they are usually so deeply humiliated when Nancy catches up with them that they spew out confessions without any urging, taking pride in having eluded her for as long as they did. Lee Zacharias, author of an unpublished paper on Nancy Drew, notes that Nancy is vain, revengeful, and competitive in her pursuit of justice, and that she wants to humiliate her enemies:

> Nancy is no mere detective. She has a compulsion to reduce her villains to broken old men. The attractive young sleuth is a ballbuster![2]

No girl sleuth is so frequently injured as Nancy. Nasty mean men are continually bopping her over the head with phallic objects, but they never get her down. She manages to dance an inspiring ballet in spite of her sprained ankle and she wins a golf tournament after spraining her hand when she topples into a flowerbed, trying to avoid slimy Mortimer Bartescue. Thus, Nancy busily fends off sexual advances, including "evil" desires in her own trusted Ned, who is always trying to get her alone in the moonlight. She runs from sex but literally chases substitute forms of "evil"—threats against property and law and order. Nancy thinks nothing of racing after a shadowy figure.

> "Dad, that man stole a purse!" Nancy whispered excitedly. "I'm going after him!"
>
> Before Mr. Drew could recover from his surprise, she had scrambled past him and was hurrying up the aisle after the thief.
>
> *The Clue in the Old Album*, p. 2

It would never occur to her that he might shoot or rape her. This restraint on realistic violence has the effect of exaggerating Nancy's power. And it underscores the contradiction: Nancy both pursues sex and runs from it.

The evil embodied in the purse-snatching, kidnapping jewel-thief gangs Nancy chases is a vaguely defined lurking force. This was precisely my understanding of evil, too, in 1951. It was always some Humbert Humbert version of a bogeyman who might hide behind bushes, or in the hayloft, or in the impenetrable darkness of the night air itself. Little girls are taught to look for evil everywhere, and to be on guard (that accounts for the contradiction, the eager defensiveness). Whenever it occurs to Nancy to look for footprints she always finds them "freshly made," like cookies, in the "soft earth." I looked for footprints until I was blue in the face. They are a lot harder to locate than one might suppose.

Nancy is out looking for evil because there are treasures to be protected. We follow clues toward something hidden, precious, and beautiful which must be defended from the greedy, disreputable tricksters. This, one supposes, is a neat Freudian analogy to the precious jewel of a girl's virginity (wonder why I didn't pick up on that in 1951? Or did I?). Often the treasure in the story is something priceless—information about a long-lost relative, an irreplaceable heirloom, or a chest of jewels. The villains are symbolic rapists who want to violate the treasure, men who haven't the proper credentials (refinement, family, education, property) to claim it. They are pushy, grabby, crude, rough, illiterate.

They are found in an assortment of Gypsies, tramps and thieves—rootless crooks and carnival clowns who have strayed from maternal and institutional influence, who want to snatch at the upper echelons of the good life. Evil is not only sexy in Nancy's universe, it's disgustingly lower class. And the men aren't just evil, they're strange. Their names tell that: Rudy Raspin, Tom Tozzle, Tom Stripe, Mr. Warte, Bushy Trott, Grumper, Alonzo Rugby, and Red Buzby. They are all good-for-nothings who want to upset the elitist WASP order. They are tricksters and hucksters who sneer at the authorities—the paternal benevolence of the businesses, institutions, and laws of the reigning upper classes.

Appearances are never deceptive in Nancy's Ivory-pure life. Good and evil are strictly white and black terms. Criminals are dark-hued and poor. One crook is "dark, with a mottled complexion and piercing black eyes." (*The Clue in the Old Album*, p. 4) This typical comic-strip crook shows up book after book:

The brim of his battered felt hat was pulled low over his forehead and the turned-up collar of his topcoat concealed his mouth and chin. But Nancy could see a pair of piercing black eyes.

The Clue of the Leaning Chimney, p. 3

Piercing dark eyes are the most common characteristic of Nancy's foes. Their greedy eyes are piercing because they are disrespectful, gazing threateningly beyond their station, perhaps seeing through the façades of the gentry whose power they crave. All the virtues of refinement, taste, intelligence, and beauty belong to Nancy's class, while everyone else is vulgar, greedy, ill-tempered, insolent. Most of them are braggarts and boasters who use aliases and bad grammar and wear wicked facial expressions. Their evil permeates the slums, which are dangerous dens of cut-throats, thugs, and thieves. When Nancy drives by, the dirty kids on the street force her to slow down, and when she is sleuthing along the waterfront, disreputable persons stare at her.

There is an even lower class in Nancy's universe, but its members rarely cross the boundaries. Nancy's housekeeper, Mrs. Gruen, is portrayed in the early books as an elderly charwoman; in later books she is Nancy's motherly confidante, but she is still a servant. Nancy feels that "To be mistaken for a housemaid was not at all flattering" (*The Clue of the Tapping Heels*, p. 146), but in *The Whispering Statue* she impersonates a maid in order to snoop in someone's room. In the first eighteen books there are seventeen Blacks—all servants.[3] They speak, grinning, in *Gone with the Wind* language, and they are often unpleasant. In *The Mystery at Lilac Inn*, Nancy interviews a servant sent from an employment agency. In despair she learns the only one they have left is "a colored woman."

> ... a more unlikely housekeeper Nancy had never seen. She
> was dirty and slovenly in appearance and had an unpleasant
> way of shuffling her feet when she walked.
>
> *The Mystery at Lilac Inn*, p. 16

Blacks are rarely villains, however. I suppose the specter
of a black man organizing a gang of jewel thieves would
have been thought by the white upper classes to be
much too unsettling and threatening for a blonde white
girl sleuth series. One of the few characters who
unnerves Nancy during her detecting career is an odd
"freckled-faced colored man who sways when he
walks."

> "Oh, you startled me!" Nancy laughed, whirling around.
> "I half expected to see a colored man leering at me."
> "Well, that's complimentary, I must say," the youth
> returned with a grin. "I'm pretty sunburned but I didn't
> know I looked as dark as that."
> Nancy told him about the missing tools and her theory
> that they had been taken by a colored person who had
> visited the house the previous day.
> "Why, I met a darky on the street yesterday!" Ned
> exclaimed.
>
> *The Clue of the Tapping Heels*, pp. 78-79

When Nancy travels to the South, she is waited on by
cheerful black servants in colonial mansions. In *The
Hidden Window Mystery* (1956) lovable old Beulah
serves squabs, sweet potatoes, corn pudding, piping hot
biscuits, and strawberry shortcake.

> When the maid left the room, Susan smiled and
> whispered to the girls, "I try to make things easier for
> Beulah but she insists upon working and serving everything
> the old-fashioned way. I must confess, though, that I love
> it."

Cliff's eyes twinkled. "Beulah's a rare person," he said. "She sort of lives in the past, and is very much like her mother, who worked for my mother. She imitates her in everything."

The Hidden Window Mystery, p. 64

In the 1930s and 1940s the series treated badly a number of other minority groups, especially Italians (swarthy gangsters) and Jews (scheming snobs). The police always had Irish names and they were blockheads, except for Nancy's kindly Chief McGinnis. Gypsies get the familiar Bobbsey treatment in Nancy Drew books, but because Gypsies are so exotic—with much romance about child-brides and mysterious violinists—Nancy is careful to distinguish between good and bad Gypsies. Gypsies embody everything any all-American straight-A girl sleuth would like to wipe off the face of the earth; but because they wear nice costumes and make beautiful music they are treated like a tourist attraction. In the original version of *The Clue in the Old Album*, which is still in print, Nancy solves a mystery for Mrs. Struthers, a fine old soul whose daughter eloped with a Gypsy. The daughter had died (retribution for her sin) and left a half-wild child for Mrs. Struthers to bring up. Nancy restores the child to her exiled father, a brilliant Gypsy violinist. Family reconciliation banishes all wildness, and Mrs. Struthers accepts the man.

Foreigners in the Nancy Drew series are either shifty-eyed sneaks or benevolent aristocrats. The shifty ones have dark, piercing eyes and are from southern Europe, while the Nordics are more beautiful and aristocratic. At the beginning of one mystery Nancy aids "an aristocratic elderly lady" who is ill and asks Nancy to take her home.

Girl sleuths can't be too careful, especially with
foreigners. But this lady's noble heart shows in her face.
"The smile with which she was rewarded immediately
erased any doubt in the girl's mind that this person
intended to bring any harm to her." (P. 3)

That story illustrates perfectly what Nancy Drew is
all about. In *The Clue in the Jewel Box* Madame
Alexandra (the foreigner with the smile) is an elegant,
exiled ex-queen, the epitome of the endangered
aristocratic tradition Nancy supports. Nancy reunites
Madame Alexandra with her long-lost grandson, who has
grown up under the name Francis Baum, without
knowing he was a prince. Baum turns out to be a bum;
he is ill-educated and has horrible manners. Ignoring
Nancy's explicit instructions to wear evening clothes, he
wears sports togs to the elegantly formal eight-course
dinner which Madame Alexandra has arranged to
celebrate his return. Soon Nancy begins to regret having
solved this mystery, because it is obvious that Francis
Baum is siphoning off the old lady's treasures. Actually,
of course, he is an impostor, but there are no proofs of
this yet, except his boorishness. Mrs. Gruen indignantly
picks up this sure clue one day when she is feeding him
lunch:

Nancy concurs. Mr. Drew, who is for giving the "prince" the benefit of the doubt, chides Nancy for her harsh judgment: "No doubt he has had to shift for himself for a long time." But Nancy isn't fooled. She knows in her heart that a real prince has innate refinement. She ultimately exposes the impostor and finds the real prince, who turns out to be a Mr. Ellington, who lives right there in River Heights. In fact, Nancy has already admired him (Mr. Ellington is SO elegant) and secretly wondered if he is perhaps the lost prince, since he has such beautiful manners. Miraculously, it turns out to be so. His identity is proven by the clue in the jewel box—the same clue that is the downfall of Francis Baum.

Thus, the original Nancy Drew series—the first thirty-five or so volumes which accumulated throughout the 1930s, 1940s, and 1950s—portrays a fading aristocracy, threatened by the restless lower classes. These are the themes which informed my childhood, when I aspired toward the delicious snobbery of Nancy's privileged life. When minorities know their place, Nancy treats them graciously. She is generous to truck drivers and cabbies and maids. But woe betide the upstarts, the dishonest social climbers who want to grab at the top.

Nancy's job is to preserve the class lines, and for her the defense of property and station are inextricably linked with purity and reputation. She defends beautiful objects, places, and treasures from violence—the sexual violence of nasty men who want to stifle her energy. There is a "proper" male authority which Nancy accepts. Almost inevitably she needs Dad or Ned to step in at the climax of the mystery to help save the treasure and rescue her from kidnappers' clutches. (" 'Oh, Dad, I thought you'd never come!' she said, snuggling in his neck." *The Clue in the Old Album*, pp. 209-210) A girl's purity and reputation are preserved, apparently, when she accedes to the protective role of the proper male authority figures. Nancy's father will protect her from sexual evil and at the right time will transfer her to the protective arms of a husband. When the good men in her life appear, the mystery is solved and all ends happily—like a wedding scene (that most respectable cover for sexual "evil") making all a girl's dreams come true.

It is a contradictory situation, of course, since the girl sleuth is in pursuit of the very world—the happy ending, the mystery solved, the symbolic wedding—she seeks to escape. According to the series' values, if Nancy were to marry she would become Mrs. Bobbsey. She already has some of Mrs. Bobbsey's dread traits: both exercise grace, charm, and cool control; the smile is their main tool; they aren't overly squeamish or weak; they are tolerant and good-humored; they laugh "good-naturedly"; they always speak words of wisdom and sympathy; they never play tricks or cavort gleefully or stomp their feet and toss their heads childishly, mussing their hair (Honey Bunch is their conscience). Mrs. Bobbsey is perfect, and to become so she has cut herself off from the action and transferred to her children the right to fun and adventure.

But Nancy Drew, as girl detective, gets to be adult without sacrificing that right to adventure. Nancy transcends the ordinary alternatives—silly Bess, ludicrous George, dull Mrs. Bobbsey. In the role of girl sleuth, Nancy, always eighteen, escapes time and enjoys the best of all worlds. She doesn't have to confront feminist anxieties. If she is as indomitable and determined as the books, say then I suspect in real life she could not become a Mrs. Bobbsey. In real life lame-brain Ned Nickerson would marry bubbly Bess, and Nancy would be a familiar feminist—frustrated and too clever to stay at home, perhaps brilliantly successful. Or maybe she would marry Ned and be sorry the next day. Ned Nickerson could never hold her down.

Cool Nancy Drew figures it is better to be locked in the timeless role of girl sleuth—forever young, forever tops, above sex, above marriage—an inspiring symbol of freedom. But was she? Once I dreamed I was a prostitute in a cream-puff shop, an old-fashioned soda shop/tea room straight out of the Nancy Drew books I had been reading. The point of the dream is not clear, since many women would argue that prostitutes are free. But I think the dream is suggestive of the ambivalence in Nancy Drew. She always has it both ways—protected and free. She is an eternal girl, a stage which is a false ideal for women in our time. Nancy's adventures take place outside time and space. Her task is to restore a crumbling place to a past and perfect order.

5

The Secret of
the Phantom Friends

"Judy, you're hopeless. You're as bad as the girls in fairy
stories who are always stealing a look at forbidden things.
Don't you ever wonder what would have happened if they
hadn't looked?"

"I don't have to wonder," Judy said. "I know. There
wouldn't have been any story."

The Forbidden Chest, p. 20

Nancy Drew's popularity meant the emergence of the
girl detective, a radical kind of heroine, it seemed. She
arrived on the scene with her magnifying glass and
flashlight, gallantly following footprints straight through
the Depression (with only the remotest clues to poverty,
despair, or war in the real world). She was above reality.
Nearly all her imitators were bountiful and beautiful,
but her closest competitor, Judy Bolton, was different.
She was almost reachable. Judy, whom I liked even
better than Nancy at age twelve, experienced the
familiar problems of being a girl, while Nancy didn't. To
me Judy was a genuine girlhood acquaintance, while
Nancy Drew was an elusive image, a mythic heroine on a
flying trapeze. Nancy succeeded because she was
extraordinarily privileged, but Judy solved mysteries

and had incredible adventures in spite of living in a rather ordinary situation in a small town with a regular family and periodic disappointments.

Most of the mass-marketed girl sleuths closely copied Nancy's myth—without having Nancy's mystique. Stratemeyer Syndicate's best-known alternatives to Nancy were Kay Tracey and the Dana Girls. Kay Tracey (by "Francis K. Judd") was less independent because she had a mother and was still in school. The Dana Girls were orphaned sister sleuths at a fancy boarding school where there was a lot of strife over curfews and playing hooky in order to trail thieves. Except for these restraints, the Danas were pale Nancy Drews of a different color (green), written by the same pseudonym. Louise and Jean Dana have had a fair following and part of the series has been recently reissued and updated: the quaint charm of the boarding school has been eclipsed by jet travel and international intrigue. It is hard to know which is a greater illusion.

In spite of the similarity, the Danas weren't so memorable as Nancy, but there were so many girl detectives looking for clues that the reader couldn't help being overwhelmed by them. Nancy and her friends made sleuthing seem like the official business of life. Nancy made it mandatory and Judy Bolton made it seem possible. I longed with all my heart to solve a mystery. I sniffed for clues like a starved sleuthhound. If only I could find a cryptic note, a lost love letter in a hollow oak, a quaint genealogical enigma behind an emerald embedded in the eye of an old figurine in the attic! I eavesdropped lustily for the secrets of thieves and searched for footprints and signet rings, but all I ever found was an old tin can and a twisted cigarette wrapper in the woods—the case of the phantom litterbugs. My playmate and I pretended to be detectives, inventing our own Nancy-style mysteries. We carried out elaborate fantasies which I cannot recall, but once my friend humored me by hiding a coded message in a hollow nook of a sycamore. We had a clue box and silver badges and we read the Girl Scout Handbook. We wrote up our findings in our notebooks.

Once a sleuth, always a sleuth. The peculiar thing is the impulse at odds: the intellectual curiosity and suspicion of the detective on the one hand, and the diligence of the fan following the rules on the other. I grew up, directed by Nancy and the Bobbseys, to follow clues and rules interchangeably. They turned me into a quiet scholar who dutifully read the book lists and did her lessons without question. I excelled in math and grammar, which were like jigsaw puzzles to me.

Basically, I suppose, I am still a girl detective. One important motif in girls' fiction is the attic—a place for girls to weep and dream and read precious letters. Jo March scribbles stories in her garret and Nancy finds treasures. Boys act out their fantasies in the outside world, but girls retreat from their regular roles in the kitchen and parlor and contemplate their secret longings. Whenever a girl sleuth encounters an attic in someone's house she immediately trots out old trunks full of photo albums, costumes, and clues. When I began writing this book, I simultaneously and coincidentally moved to an old farmhouse with a mysterious attic, and I know that in my secret mind I have since been thinking about secret panels and hidden treasure. While my conscious mind has informed me that the family who lived here for generations was so poor that lost treasures in hidey holes are unlikely, I have not been able to stop snooping. And, sure enough, underneath a floorboard in the attic I found a surprise. Resting in the hollow between the beams was a dusty cloth bundle, about the size of a hobo's baggage. My old sleuthing instincts surfaced, but with them came a feeling of dread. I expected the bundle to contain a dead baby, something Nancy Drew never thought of. If it wasn't a dead baby, then it was arsenic somebody couldn't get rid of—even while the girl sleuth in me hoped for a gold doubloon. I took the bundle outside and cut it apart carefully, shaking off the dust. It was a collection of little rags wound tightly together and stuffed in an old stocking, knotted at the opening. I took it apart, rag by rag, and there was nothing. It was a granny-bundle, a little old lady's ragbag. The real mystery was why somebody tied up some rags so sweetly and tucked them under the floorboard, but that wasn't the way it would have happened in a Nancy Drew story.

> Nancy took the knife and pried off two tiny screws. The face then dropped down into her hands.
>
> "Oh!" she cried. "The secret compartment! I've found it!"
>
> She had expected to view the "works" of the clock, but instead beheld a round metal box which fit snugly into the wall. The clock was only a clever sham. To her delight, she found that the metal box could be removed from the wall. . . .
>
> She fumbled with the catch on the box and lifted the lid. There before her was an array of jewels such as she had never viewed before in her life. Brilliant diamonds mounted in old-fashioned rings and quaint bracelets. Pendants of rubies and brooches of sapphires. For a moment, Nancy Drew was so dazzled by the display that she could only stare open-mouthed.
>
> *The Mystery at Lilac Inn*, pp. 188-189

And it didn't happen that way in Judy Bolton mysteries either, when Judy looked under the floorboard.

There, hidden between the beams was a vase in the shape of a tree. A beautiful woman was leaning against the trunk, a woman who looked like a goddess. Her drapes tapered upward as though blown by the wind and above her head Judy saw the pink of apple blossoms. . . .

The Invisible Chimes, p. 153

Childhood looms even larger. The old farmhouse where I now live is in Pennsylvania, and when I began looking back to my childhood literature, I soon became aware that I was living in the region of Pennsylvania where Judy Bolton solved mysteries. When I read Nancy again, the old hunger for tea and cakes in roadside inns returned, and so did the desire to go sneaking around with a magnifying glass looking for secret panels. But while I did not recover many specific memories of Nancy's personality or adventures, every detail of Judy Bolton's life came swirling back when I read her stories again. My fondness for Judy's very full world was rejuvenated: her cat Blackberry, her brother Horace who had a parrot that said naughty words to Blackberry, Horace's coffee-colored car, Judy sitting in the latticed porch learning French with her friend Honey, her wonderful old house with a round attic window, the invisible chimes under the floorboard, the devotion between Peter and Judy—not the gooey kind of romance I would have detested (or the sterile convenience of Nancy and Ned's relationship), but a healthy, appreciative, equal exchange of feelings. Judy had red hair and was slightly temperamental, but the two facts, astonishingly, were never correlated. She had a questioning, uninhibited mind, she had a definite and complex relationship to a place and a family—and she had a secret clue drawer in her antique desk.

As soon as I started re-reading my girlhood books, it became apparent to me that books like the timeless, unchanging, mythic, unreachable Bobbsey Twins were written in an office somewhere. It was equally apparent that Margaret Sutton, the author of Judy Bolton books, was an individual author. Her books had dedications: "To Dorothy," "To My Cousin Clella, Who Shared a Part of the Real Adventure," "To Peggy and Eleanor." Reading Judy Bolton, one feels intimate with her and with her author. Nancy Drew's author is also a real person, but Nancy Drew books are laid out like black-and-white vinyl floor tiles. The pattern overrides characterization and depth. Margaret Sutton says she wrote the first few Judy Bolton stories before Nancy Drew appeared on the market, but Grosset & Dunlap hemmed and hawed for a few years before accepting the series—until the girl detective was a certain success.[1] By 1932, when the first Judy Bolton books were published, Nancy Drew was selling like flapjacks. Judy Bolton books are original in substance, but they have an overlay of familiar mystery paraphernalia: clues, crooks, spooks, and all.

In spite of the way Judy was fitted into a popular pattern, I found as a child—and still feel, as I pore over my faded copies of *The Clue in the Patchwork Quilt* and *The Secret of the Musical Tree*—that Judy Bolton was more satisfying and substantial, and more provoking, than any of the other girl detectives. While I suspect there is some prejudice, some keepsake in my soul that I won't let go, I can't help thinking that Judy was preferable to her sister sleuths, though she surely falls short of feminist hopes for young heroines and can be censured by feminists on several counts. Perhaps by arguing for her virtues in this chapter, I can better illustrate the spectrum of "pop pap." I think Sutton strives toward Louisa May Alcott's verisimilitude; far more than shallow sentiment leads girls between ten and fourteen to re-read *Little Women* ritually each year with a bursting heart, for Louisa May Alcott was an excellent writer and her feminism moved her pen. I'm inclined to believe that because Margaret Sutton thought of herself as a genuine author instead of a commercial writer, and because she lovingly crafted her series, she succeeded in instilling that old wash-and-wear girl sleuth pattern with more humanity than the others did. And Sutton, who has never found in adult literature the satisfaction and charm of children's literature, takes Judy Bolton seriously. The series has been a major part of her life, and she currently goes about collecting old sets of Judy books from second-hand stores for her grandchildren. She also deeply believes in the series form. When she was ten she was so disappointed to learn that there was no sequel to *The Secret Garden* that she vowed that someday she would write a series of stories all about one character so that other children would not have to suffer the same disappointment. She wrote thirty-eight books, one a year until Grosset & Dunlap canceled the series in 1967.

Judy Bolton lives in a mountainous region of Pennsylvania which seems to have more than its share of blackmailers and kidnappers. In the first book Judy is fifteen and longing for excitement: "All her life Judy had pined for a mystery to solve." (*The Vanishing Shadow*, p. 7) Judy's ambitions are born out of the familiar frustrations of growing up female. She wishes she were a boy so she can be a detective:

"A great one who goes into all kinds of dangers. I wouldn't mind that—afterwards. There would be the thrill of finding out things. You can't imagine what a satisfaction there is in hitting on a real live clue."

The Vanishing Shadow, p. 53

After Judy wins a reputation as an amateur detective, friends say, "Judy wouldn't be Judy if she didn't find a mystery to solve." (*The Riddle of the Double Ring*, p. 209) In an early adventure, *The Ghost Parade*, Judy is fuming because her brother Horace is going to have all the fun chasing counterfeiters while she is packed off to camp. She vows to show him up and does. The crooks conveniently hide out near her camp and she and Blackberry catch them. (Blackberry is one major male in her life—an independent tom who turns up crucial clues, when he is not getting lost or being cat-napped.)

Although Judy matures, she remains steadfast on one point: she will never give up, she will seek adventure, she will find the truth, no matter where it leads. I think I identified with her precisely because of that insistence of hers. Nancy Drew never needed to assert her identity—she had only to invoke the magical name of her famous father; she was granted complete assurance because her scene was timeless and perfect. Nancy was remote but Judy was inspiring, for within a context of growth and change it was up to her to fight for her right to be herself. That was very important to me—and at odds with my Bobbsey obedience—the insistence that I could do what the world told me I could not. Nancy blurred my eyes with longing, but Judy invigorated me.

Judy is not in the least glamorous or dainty. She is more interested in her intellect than in her looks. She grows up during the series, which covers her life between ages fifteen and twenty-two. At first she is impressed by the high-school moneyed clique. The Farringdon-Pett mansion awes her and the name sounds "royal." She envies blonde, aristocratic Lorraine Lee and is snowed by Arthur Farringdon-Pett into accepting an engagement ring. (She wonders why "being engaged to him wasn't as thrilling as she had thought it was going to be." *The Riddle of the Double Ring*, p. 50) Arthur turns out to be dull and Lorraine is stuck up. "Lorraine's studied mannerisms prevented her from enjoying life as completely as Judy did." (*The Ghost Parade*, p. 47) Since Arthur wants a girl who will stay prettily put, he chooses china-doll Lorraine and Judy marries plain Peter Dobbs, who doesn't inhibit her with demands for docility. "He liked detecting as well as she did. There would always be mysteries to solve while they were together." (*The Rainbow Riddle*, p. 10) When she has a bridal shower, she wishes she didn't have to go. On perhaps the only occasion when she goes to tea, she says afterward, "I thought they'd keep us there sipping tea and eating sandwiches forever." (*The Forbidden Chest*, p. 82) Judy is an individualist who doesn't give a hoot about housecleaning, can't sew, and can just barely bake a gooseberry pie. She's more comfortable chasing a blackmailer named Blackie or sniffing clues with her cat Blackberry.

Judy is more real than the syndicate sleuths or Nancy Drew because she has to fight male chauvinism. Nancy Drew's "liberation"—and Nancy does have far greater freedom—spurs escapist fantasy because Nancy is above the problem altogether. The reader escapes to dreamland where she expends her imaginative energies, and then returns (sometimes crashing) to an entirely different reality. But Judy is both protected and challenged by the male world with which she manages to cope, and against which she jousts—with wits, not Wonder Girl advantages. Nancy finesses feminist issues and has daddy, car, and money enough to avoid them, while Judy solves mysteries as an independent girl detective in spite of the limitations forced upon her by society. Her struggles potentially strengthen the reader's determination to be free.

It is a significant failing of the series that Judy doesn't have a career or role other than that of amateur detecting, so that she gets energy and direction from male approval, which is sometimes condescending. Usually, though, her husband, brother, and father—all busy men—treat her seriously and as an equal. Peter is an FBI man; Horace is a reporter; her father is a doctor, saving lives right and left; Arthur is an important architect, toting around blueprints in his airplane. Horace is sickly and sissy and shy before he becomes the town hero by warning people about the dam breaking—but Judy predicted that flood and was the brains and initiative behind Horace's heroism. As a result, Horace attains his manhood and becomes a hot-shot reporter. But it is Judy's daring exploits that supply his scoops, in book after book.

All this comes close to suggesting that Judy, like unnumbered females before and since, finds herself serving as fodder for male egos: a woman standing behind her man. But while Judy takes some pleasure from providing this service, she refuses to reconcile herself to it. When I was twelve she was one of my hopes for survival. She was taken seriously for simply doing what she was capable of doing.

Unfortunately, her only strong models are men. When Judy goes to Washington she tours awesome white buildings, but Peter deals with FBI business. Judy is fascinated by the immense statues of men in the Capitol, which soon begin to make her feel creepy.

> She turned, nearly bumping into a protruding marble foot. The one statue of a woman among all those honored men seemed to stare down at her, disapproving of her clumsy behavior.
>
> *The Whispered Watchword*, p. 46

The statue is a likeness of Frances E. Willard, the founder of the Women's Christian Temperance Union.

While there are few heroines in Judy's universe, her father, who praises her "unusual powers of deduction," is an important guide for her. He is forever saying, "Use your head, Judy girl."

> Once she started using her head, as her father so often advised her, she was no longer frightened—just curious.
> *The Clue in the Ruined Castle*, p. 87

Judy's mother, conforming to girls' series requirements, is barely present. (" 'Dinner is on the table,' announced Mrs. Bolton when she could be heard." *The Mark on the Mirror*, p. 13) Mothers are not models of liberation for the adolescent mystery fan, and Judy is determined to do unusual things with spirit and courage.

Judy's determination to solve mysteries is different from Nancy Drew's crisp, efficient methods of reducing the world to a clean, quaint tea room. I remember how strongly I identified with Judy Bolton's wonder. To her, the puzzle was more thrilling than the solution.

> This time it never occurred to Judy that the voice might be anything ordinary. She didn't think of common things when she tried to figure it out. Instead she thought of faked spirit voices, timed bombs, a ventriloquist, perhaps, and secret messages.
> *The Voice in the Suitcase*, pp. 18-19

That Judy has to conjure up possibilities shows an active resistance to her limitations. But such extremes as Judy imagines happen to Nancy Drew unannounced: Nancy is the passive recipient of both luxury and danger.

The Bolton series seems to suggest that manhood is the only alternative for girls who reject the traditional household role. And it is contradictory, of course, for girls like Judy are struggling against a male-dominated system which strives to keep women in the kitchen. Like Nancy, Judy lapses into the protective embrace of the Good Men in her life. Judy's dilemma—her indomitable spirit vs. society's restraints—is dramatized, overly so, by the fact that her husband is an FBI agent, obsessed with secrecy and importance.

> An FBI agent had to have privacy and his wife should not be the curious type. Just the same, Judy was curious.
>
> *The Secret of the Sand Castle*, p. 3

But Judy goes her own route:

> "Yes, I know. My duties as the wife of an FBI agent were made quite clear to me when we were in Washington. I'm supposed to be a good housewife, with home and family my chief concern. I can keep pets and raise flowers and conduct myself like a model citizen, but never, no never, may I get myself involved in any of your assignments. Anyway," Judy finished airily, "I have my own mystery to solve . . ."
>
> *The Secret of the Sand Castle*, p. 5

Usually Judy's mystery turns out to be the same case Peter is working on and she solves it for him. Peter Dobbs, with his FBI calling card and revolver, is, at age twenty-five, as tough as Joe Friday. He frequently bounds in for the rescue and roundup, but sometimes Judy rescues him. Peter is conveniently absent most of the time, intruding only to give the reader a sense of Judy's security or to help Judy in a jam. Unfortunately, Peter is a pallid personality and the FBI is a looming megalith of male power. The result is both to enlarge male supremacy and to congratulate Judy for standing up to it.

And her marriage does not end her life. Marriage gives Judy confidence and freedom, if anything. It certainly doesn't inhibit her, in spite of Mr. FBI and his secrets. She insists she is "still the same red-haired, adventure-loving girl she had always been." (*The Forbidden Chest*, p. 2) As her wedding approaches, she tries to restrain herself from getting into scrapes, thinking that mature married women don't go around solving mysteries, but that's only an old tale she's heard. She literally can't help herself. She is hot on the trail of a mystery the week before the ceremony. She loses the box containing her wedding dress in a haunted house and is almost blown up by a bomb at her reception. A crook chase nicely detracts attention from the connubial stuff going on during Judy's honeymoon, spent at a series of quaint inns, which are really fronts for a smuggling ring.

Although Sutton lapses into many stereotypes about marriage, she does make it seem natural and normal, except for the implausibility of the FBI role. She stresses that marriage doesn't mean the end of aspirations and life and everything good and real. And she doesn't falsify marriage as something so glorious that the reality can only be a disappointment. Judy's marriage is not fully characterized because of pale Peter, but it is a plain and friendly, mutually protective situation in which the partners can go on being human. Margaret Sutton confronts head-on the conventional notion that marriage means the end of adventure for a girl—an assumption on which most series books are built—and shows Judy persisting with spirit in pursuit of adventures. That she and the other girl detectives have to *pursue* adventures, rather than freely involving themselves in meaningful activity, is revealing.

Judy's mysteries are often about counterfeiters and blackmailers and other FBI extravaganzas, but some recent stories probe more realistic wrongdoings: real estate swindles, propaganda, quack psychiatry, juvenile delinquency, alcoholism. One book exposes the propagandistic power of a right-wing youth group. Judy triumphs over crudities, cover-ups, ego-trips. The greatest wrongs are those that blind and hurt individuals. The books value order, a sense of place, balance, tolerance, rationality, self-knowledge, sympathy. Judy is critical of artificiality and appreciative of quality. The original Nancy Drew series, among others, values power, supremacy, conquest, property, and privilege—under the wholesome aegis of the conquest of evil. Judy Bolton books are more delicate, more attuned to individual human possibilities—the values shine through the stereotypes. The two series have different sensibilities, despite their apparent similarities.

Another basic difference between the two is that in spite of the mystery form, Judy is a liberal. I think Arthur Prager is quite mistaken in his nostalgic survey of children's literature, *Rascals at Large*, when he says Judy is "politically far to the right of Nancy," basing his observation on a scene in *The Mysterious Half-Cat* in which Judy talks about how dreadful it must be to be poor, and how poverty can breed crime. He didn't mention the endless associations between poverty and evil in the Nancy Drew books throughout the 1930s, and the confusion of deprivation with shiftlessness, a repugnant source of evil. In one Judy Bolton book, Judy is responsible for ending the posh/poor dividing line between upper and lower Grove Street, challenging and eradicating the local prejudices against the mill workers and helping to improve housing conditions. Judy's sense of justice is not merely ghetto law and order: there is some understanding of motivation and circumstance. In Nancy Drew books, where good and evil are clearly delineated, there is no sympathy for wrongdoers.

I have the impression that Margaret Sutton could have been a far stronger writer if Judy could have solved puzzles that had fewer counterfeiters, doubles, heists, and shysters—old-hat characters in plots that hardly stretch the imagination. Sutton sacrifices her imagination by accommodating the mystery genre to her capacity for wonder, which she translates into Judy's unboxable curiosity. On the other hand, perhaps the odd combination—mystery formula and individual consciousness—saved the series from excessive sentimentality. Judy's liberal outlook is at odds with the basically conservative format, and the result is ambiguous, whereas the Nancy Drew series is built on a clean, neat paradox.

Criticism of Nancy Drew and praise for Judy Bolton must be qualified, of course. The girl detectives have had an enormous influence on women's lives, in ways both good and bad. Their "liberation" was inspiring—at last females were getting credit—but it wasn't enough, and sometimes their liberation was deceptive. But it seems to me that the Judy Bolton series comes closest to containing realism, psychological depth, and honest values within the girls' mystery form. There are actual themes—the small-town girl moving to a city, the problems of urbanization and relocation, the discovery of the meaning of one's past, the quest for identity—and enough fantasy and aspiration to stimulate children. As light entertainment, the series is less damaging, I suspect, than most escapist literature. And I think its central ambiguity results from its struggle to be something more than that. Within the bounds of my subject—the relative freedom of the girl sleuths—the Judy Bolton series is more friendly to feminists, although on the surface the Nancy Drew series might appear to be.

Just Plain Trixie

Judy Bolton and all the original girl detectives of the 1930s and 1940s are going out of print, all except the strong Stratemeyer stars—Nancy Drew and her twin satellites, the Dana Girls—and one other, an adolescent who has quietly held her place on the revolving racks in dime stores. Trixie Belden stars in an unpretentious series of sixteen mysteries, published in cheap hardbacks by Whitman Co. Trixie was one of my favorites, and she was closer to my age and situation than the others.

Like the Judy Bolton stories, Trixie Belden mysteries are slightly off key, although the central ingredients of the recipe are obvious. Trixie is poor and her best friend next door is rich, with a mansion, horses, a groom, a governess, a limousine—the works. Trixie has to stay home and hoe the garden a lot, but her life is enriched when the Wheelers move into the mansion up the road. As it turns out, Trixie's initial awe of wealth evaporates.

> "Oh, Moms, I'm so glad I was born into this family. I feel so sorry for people like Honey. . . . Honey just never seems to have any fun with her father and mother the way Bobby and Brian and Mart and I do. I'm so glad we're not rich."
>
> "So am I," Mrs. Belden said with a smile. "It's much more fun to work for the things you want than to have them given to you on a silver platter."
>
> *The Secret of the Mansion*, pp. 140-141

Thank goodness the Trixie Belden series insisted that the rich weren't happy. It is possible that what depth there was in the Judy Bolton books and the self-congratulation of the Trixie Belden books saved me from pining away into a shadow, longing for Bobbsey heaven. The Trixie stories had a healthy, restraining effect. They held up no glamorous ideals and weren't calculated to make an ordinary little girl unhappy. What they did do was unfairly use Honey and her mansion to work up a hunger for class and privileges—and did so, paradoxically, in order to reinforce middle- and lower-to-middling class values.

I cherished the first three volumes of the Trixie Belden series (written between 1948 and 1951 by Julie Campbell; some of the later books were by Kathryn Kenny). They were full of rich natural detail not present in any of the other books. They made living in the country seem all right, even if they did make me wish there was a rich girl with horses up the road a piece. Recently I read the remainder of the series to find out what happened and I found a certain wholesomeness sustained throughout, although the mystery form has a built-in preposterousness—an incredible number of crooks and jewels—and the pop format, however modified, can be seen below the surface.

In the first book Trixie longs for excitement and a horse. She lives way out in the country with nothing to do but chores. Soon after the book begins the rich people arrive in answer to her wish, and the daughter is Trixie's age. Trixie is a tomboy, and so she is at first disenchanted with pale, thin Honey Wheeler. Honey is a starched little fraidy-cat who has nightmares and is scared of every bug and weed she sees. But Trixie urges Honey through some adventures and within two days they are bosom pals and Honey is eating like a pig and getting "brown as a berry." In the second book they go traveling in a fine red trailer, chasing after a beautiful red-haired boy who has run away from his cruel stepfather. They want to let him know he has inherited an estate from his uncle. Honey likes the boy, Jim, so much that she wants him for a brother and so her daddy adopts him.

Honey's mamma is a socialite who has no time for her daughter, a fact which saddens Honey in every single book. Honey suspects her mother wanted a boy and was disappointed in having a girl. Honey's orphan-like state strengthens the role of Trixie's "Moms," who is warm and wise and wonderful, an archetypal, beatific slave-wife who's so busy caring lovingly for her children and baking pies that she has no time to worry about society. Wealth can't buy the satisfaction of cooking and canning, as Trixie wisely observes.

> "You're right, Honey. I'd hate to have a lot of servants cluttering up our place. And nobody could possibly cook as well as Moms does. The funny part of it is that she never makes a big fuss about it, either. When she dons an apron she looks younger and prettier than ever, and she sort of wanders into the kitchen and wanders out again with an enormous meal."
>
> *The Mysterious Visitor*, p. 19

(Trixie doesn't have any intention of following in her mother's footsteps, of course.) Honey is the poor little rich girl, with all those servants hulking about. Honey doesn't even have any blue jeans to wear.

> Honey appeared, then, in an immaculate white riding habit and russet boots so shiny you could see your face in them.
> *The Secret of the Mansion*, p. 33

"Goodness knows, I can't have any fun unless I'm wearing jeans," says Trix. (*The Mysterious Visitor*,

p. 35) As soon as Honey gets some jeans they start having adventures, hoping to open up the Belden-Wheeler Detective Agency when they are grown. One of their first mysteries involves another poor little rich girl, Diana Lynch, who had worn jeans until her father got rich. Trixie and Honey rush in and save her from a swarm of servants, especially the butler "with his silly old silver tray." (*The Mysterious Visitor*, p. 188) Di gets jeans again and joins Trixie's club.

Trixie is an adolescent (aged thirteen) who is determined to be neither child nor female—or feminine, at least. You can picture a tanned, freckled, snub-nosed, frizzy-haired kid who's no longer a ruffled "little girl" and hardly a teenager and not yet a "young lady"—simply a "kid." In that embarrassing transition period, the world is full of rules and roles one has to resist. Trixie is sharp and shrewd, but if she tries to think some adult says, "Don't think. Every time you do, this place is swarming with state troopers and G-men." (*The Mysterious Visitor*, p. 84). With domineering older brothers and the responsibility of helping care for a toddler brother, she is determinedly independent. She does her stuff anyway, despite their hoots, and adults and brothers come around to confessing their confidence in her.

> They were used to Trixie's bursts of enthusiasm, and they always paid attention to her. Life with her might be exasperating at times, but it was never dull. She had led them into and out of some mighty thrilling episodes.
> *The Mystery at Bob-White Cave*, p. 18

Each book centers on her acts of heroism, and the boys do very little. She goes down a rope over a cliff to rescue a girl caught in a bush; she descends into a sink-hole in a dark cave to collect some rare fish and is almost swept away by a tide; she rescues her brother from a wildcat; she saves the forest from poachers; she gets kidnapped. Her brothers tease her about being unfeminine. They say she handles a needle like it's a crowbar. But Trixie says, "As far as I'm concerned, all sewing is cross-stitching, because every time I look a needle in the eye I feel cross." (*The Mysterious Visitor*, p. 15)

Trixie bristles at being referred to as "just a girl." She is impatient and impulsive, and she excitedly jumps to conclusions (usually correct). The books more or less accede to male/female stereotypes, but for a change twist them and congratulate the female. Though Trixie is excitable, she is also practical. She has no illusions about good times in the big time. She doesn't care for fantasy, but is firmly rooted in the garden soil of the back yard. She doesn't even go for fairy tales.

> "I know, you're afraid she'll turn us into gingerbread dolls! Or is that the way the story goes in 'Hansel and Gretel'?" Trixie was never sure of her facts about fairy tales.
>
> *The Marshland Mystery*, p. 64

Trixie knows the value of work, and though she complains about her chores she knows they must be done. She saves for a horse and works on projects for her secret club, the Bob-Whites. Although some of the members are rich, the rule is that all club money must be earned. The club works on charity projects to aid UNICEF, crippled kids, orphans, earthquake victims, etc. There is so much work going on that it's a wonder Trixie gets her mysteries solved. But her chores teach her responsibility. When she sees a shiny bike left in the mud, she deplores the carelessness of the owner.

Trixie's home is like the farm as I knew it: a vegetable garden with endless weeds, a big warm mom in the kitchen canning catsup and beans, and the lurking fear of snakes and wild animals—a world far removed from the civilized security of the Bobbseys. Trixie's garden chores are demanding and she is knowledgeable about her work. She weeds with her scratcher, throws scratch to the chickens, pulls out the purslane, hills up the potatoes, and waters the tomato seedlings.

Trixie understands weather and weeds and wild animals. There are more descriptive passages in these books than in any other popular series I know, and there is careful attention to natural settings. The authors write indulgently about the wildlife and forests of Rip van Winkle country—Trixie's Hudson River region. Trixie and her Bob-White friends ride their horses into the forest and they know every trail and danger. They never go anyplace without their flashlights. Nature is the real world to be dealt with, and social evils are seen in that perspective. The wilderness is present in abundant detail in every book.

The preserve was the place the Bob-Whites liked best to ride. It was deep, dark, and mysterious, with trails crossing and recrossing. There were parts of it, still unexplored, where deer and foxes roamed. On rare occasions even a catamount found its way down from the Catskills. The west boundary ended only ten feet from the edge of the great bluffs that hung over the Hudson River.

The Mystery of the Missing Heiress, p. 19

In the last book of the series to date, the great industrial swoop threatens a marshland which is a favorite wild haunt, where Trixie and her friends go to find herbs for botany class—tansy, boneset, bergamot, pennyroyal. When Trixie goes on a trip to another region, there is considerable attention to the setting. This is in the Ozarks.

> Limestone ledges made a serrated pattern down to Ghost River, which emptied into the huge basin of Lake Wamatosa. Pines, walnuts, hickories, butternuts, papaws, dogwoods, redbuds, and wild crab apple trees tangled, in dense clumps, with wild grapevines and spiraling woodbines.
>
> *The Mystery at Bob-White Cave*, p. 22

There is no commentary on the scenery; it is just factual notation, given because it is important—given in particularity, unlike the generalized settings through which Nancy Drew floats. Nancy settings are quaint and thrilling. Trixie brought me down to earth and made the natural, real world inviting. *The Mystery at Bob-White Cave* is full of details (nearly enough to counteract its stereotyped pictures of happy hillfolk quilting and feuding), details such as these: eating wild poke greens and canned squirrel; the rain crows crying rain; gathering ginseng and herbs; making blackberry preserves; driving mules and wagons on treacherous backwoods trails.

The Trixie Belden series stresses work and thrift and plainness and energy, though it does so in a typically seductive fashion, with its emphasis on WASP-centered wealth. But the books are relatively plausible mystery-adventures about a group of energetic kids doing some healthful things.

It's perhaps a good thing I didn't read beyond volume three when I was a child. The later books show Trixie jetting off on impossible vacations, even though her trips are usually to the un-exotic Midwest—the Ozarks, the Mississippi River, an Iowa sheep farm, places where Trixie still has to do quite ordinary chores. In recent books Honey has become "a tall, graceful blonde" and the club is getting its own station wagon, a spaceship is being launched, and New York City is closer. And Trixie is saying, "Too many people are running down our country and everyone in it, with a special hate for teenagers. I like us. I like all of us." (*The Mystery of the Missing Heiress*, p. 23) The stories are repetitious, one reason series books by definition leave a bad taste in educators' mouths. And later books are less complex; Trixie's mind seems to have shrunk somewhat.

But among the girl sleuths, Trixie is (or was) one of the most liberating. The values of the books—threaded as they are with girl detective plot fibers—are superior to the Bobbsey values of many a series. The simplistic psychology of the characters, situations, and themes must be held up against the utter emptiness of the syndicated series, in which there is no psychological dimension. If I were discussing literary values, I would have no subject, but I'm talking about popular dreams, and the relative damage of indoctrination, and within that context I've become a connoisseur.

6

The Glamour Girls

There was another style of sleuthing. Some girl detectives had official careers—up in the clouds, in the movies, in busy hospitals and ad agencies. They were efficient and capable and free. But although they had their choice of romance and vista, they were in some ways the most limited of the detective heroines. Their careers fell far short of what women were capable of, and they were in fact only obedient servants to male chiefs—so they found more excitement in solving mysteries than in the glamour of their jobs. The girl sleuth, it seems, was a comfortable fictional role that siphoned female energy away from more revolutionary ambitions. And the women writers of these series always acquiesced to male authorities, the economics of the commercially successful formula.

Although the Dana Girls were not career girls, but students, a scene from one of their adventures (*The Secret of the Swiss Chalet*) illustrates a recurring theme in girls' mysteries, useful for introducing the glamorous career-girl detectives. When the Dana Girls go to Switzerland, they visit a quaint Swiss chalet with colorfully decorated, carved wooden furniture, and they go to a folk festival of gaily garbed peasants. Swiss cheese and chocolate and watches play peekaboo in the narrative. Louise and Jean wear leather shorts and carry Swiss chocolate bars on their mountain climbs. (Louise and Jean wouldn't be caught dead in leather shorts at their boarding school.) They ski on precarious mountain peaks and are rescued from an avalanche by a St. Bernard (Brutus) with a barrel around his neck. They feast on *koenigsberger klops* and pear bread. The reader is even given the recipes.

Such stories realize the authorized, glamorized dreams of our culture perfectly. Things happen in series fiction the way they are supposed to happen in regular, clockwork reality. If Nancy Drew went to the Himalayas she would no doubt encounter the Abominable Snowman, who would turn out to be Bushy Trott in disguise, for the fantastic cannot happen. One job the girl sleuth has is to go around with a broom dispelling the supernatural, like brushing cobwebs and magic out of life. Decades of American writers have been obsessed with the mysteries of evil and the supernatural, suspicious of the human capacity for reason. But in popular children's literature, life is simple and safe: there are no real mysteries.

Once upon a time when the Outdoor Girls motored to Cape Cod, there was a breathtaking fantasy image of what Cape Cod would be like.

> Cape Cod! What a world of romantic pictures the mere name evokes.
>
> Back in Deepdale, when the bungalow at Seascape had first been mentioned, all the girls could think of was the joy of meeting personally the rugged, quaint, picturesque type of old sea captain so humorously and humanly portrayed in story books and novels and to see the quaint Cape towns and fishing villages, with which, through their reading, they felt so well acquainted.
>
> *The Outdoor Girls on Cape Cod*, pp. 22-23

This tourist mentality pervades the career-sleuth stories. They are sources of my own appetite for souvenirs of glamour. When I went to Cape Cod in 1963 I dutifully read an illustrated guidebook and marveled at the quaintness of the winding streets of arty shops, and the first roadside clam joint I inspected had Patti Page singing "Old You-Know-What" on the jukebox like an official theme song. The snobs were complaining about the tourists, but to me it was the image that counted— the image of sea captains, sea food, sea artists.

The career girl sleuths pursued these romantic pictures. Cape Cod, Acapulco, tourist homes on a rocky Maine coast, volcanoes in Hawaii, mosses in old manses. They were dressed-up substitutes for grander ambitions. Nursing was glamorous, but serious female ambitions to be doctors were channeled into a role of "helpfulness" and "efficiency." Every career girl solved mysteries on the job, something male doctors, astronomers, and lawyers had no time to do. It was a tacit admission that the careers of women were not important enough in themselves. Interest shifted to landscape, secrets, problems, clues.

Cherry Ames, Vicki Barr, Connie Blair, and Beverly Gray are the glamour girls I remember best from my childhood. They were published by Grosset & Dunlap, and although these series were written by individual women, it is hard to distinguish them from the polished formulas of many of the others.

The Beverly Gray "College Mysteries," begun in 1934 by Clair Blank, included four introductory books about Beverly in college (including some adventures with Gypsies), followed by twenty-one books about the mysteries she solved as a journalist in New York. The series lingered over the typical romantic settings so alluring in girl detective books.

The snow-covered gabled roof of Mountain View Lodge was visible over the crest of the hill, and as they drew nearer the girls could see that the building was immense. It was a two-story, dark brown house, and the trees and shrubbery surrounding the long drive and the house were bent low under the still falling snow.

"Christmas!" Lenora murmured. "It looks just like a Christmas card, trees covered with white, lights shining through the snow."

Beverly Gray's Problem, p. 82

The girls drive up to the lodge in a sleigh, and inside they find supper waiting before an open fire.

An important motif in girls' series books is the arrival at the quaint destination, a carryover from comfortable British novels. The characters reach the end of their journey and find all the comforts of home, but in a different and delightful setting. Often there is food waiting and a fire blazing and the bed covers are turned back. There is ecstasy in being securely at home in the uncertain outside. Thus adventure is an illusion, the unknown is reduced to the familiar.

Although there was a surplus of sentiment in the Beverly Gray stories, there were appealing elements.

Beverly was a born dreamer, and now she gave herself up entirely to her bright daydreams. She wanted to be a writer after college.

Beverly Gray, Sophomore, p. 52

In particular, I identified with Beverly's unabiding ambition and independence.

There was a driving ambition in her heart that would not let her idle her life away.

Beverly Gray on a Treasure Hunt, p. 157

When Beverly writes a play she works so industriously that she has to take a rest cure for her exhaustion.

> Idleness was hard on Beverly. She had never been one to waste time, to squander precious minutes doing nothing. Now, with hours forced upon her and the means to fill them taken away, she was at a loss trying to find things to do . . . she felt time heavy on her hands.
>
> *Beverly Gray's Problem*, p. 75

No girl sleuth idles. A girl sleuth is a perfect product of the Protestant production panic. Beverly's career is more important than love or looks. On a world cruise she writes daily:

> She was not letting any time slip idly through her fingers. Every story she wrote and sold now was another brick in making solid the foundation of her career. She might have sold a novel, but she did not intend to rest on any laurels that might bring her. She had her eye on bigger and better things and she intended to go after them.
>
> *Beverly Gray on a Treasure Hunt*, p. 19

Beverly's ambition buys glamour. In the first few pages of one book these items appear casually: Beverly Gray interviewing a celebrity for the *Tribune*; lunch at a New York restaurant; life in a New York apartment; the theater; Fifth Avenue shops; clothes; jewels; and movies. Beverly and her friends go to a fancy party.

> It was the sort of affair the girls had often read about. There were beautifully gowned women, sparkling with jewels, men, darkly handsome in evening clothes, enchanting music and laughter.
>
> *Beverly Gray's Problem*, pp. 19-20

And if they are not in New York, they are cruising off to some exotic port. While in the Orient Beverly becomes a war correspondent, covering the war in China:

> An assignment to cover the War! Excitement tingled in her fingertips. She visualized it as flags flying, bands blaring, military music and the tramp of marching feet. The sun would sparkle on shiny helmets. There would be people cheering the marching thousands. Of course somewhere distant would be the actual fighting. But that would be very remote.
>
> *Beverly Gray on a Treasure Hunt*, p. 167

The Beverly Gray mysteries are thinly plotted compared to the skillful webs of the Nancy Drews. Sometimes the mystery is solved halfway through the book, and the ending is a pieced-together assortment of episodes. But there is adventure galore. *Beverly Gray's Problem* includes a flood, a plane crash, a series of jewel robberies, the theft of blueprints, a ski accident, a blizzard, and pneumonia, all interlaced with the glamour of a hit play, parties, romances, and reporting assignments. During the series Beverly is captured by cannibals and by a hermit lunatic. She is frequently in plane disasters, floods, locked closets, and dungeons. She is wounded in the war in Shanghai and heroically keeps it a secret, nearly dying of infection.

Romance is interspersed with the action. Beverly's ambiguous engagement to Larry Owens, a mysterious flying secret agent, is sustained throughout the series. In one book she can't choose between Jim and Larry (we're not sure of the difference) and *Beverly Gray's Challenge* concerns her jealousy. She and Larry bail out of a plane into a volcano and are so excited over surviving that he kisses her impulsively and she doesn't notice. Once out of the volcano they go on an innocent all-night idyll together in Hawaii. But romances are secrets. Even with her best friends Beverly doesn't discuss her romantic feelings (or her war wounds). They don't gossip; one of the highest values in these books is privacy. Her best friend Shirley gets engaged before Beverly is sure the couple like each other. Shirley is a famous actress consumed by her love of the stage—until Mr. Right intrudes. Beverly surmises that Shirley will abandon her career in order to cook breakfast for her husband.

> As for herself, Beverly knew nothing would supplant her urge to write. That was a part of her. But writing was something that would not interfere with married life—at least not as much as acting. No matter where she went Beverly could take her ambition and working materials with her. That gave her a happy satisfaction.
>
> *Beverly Gray on a Treasure Hunt*, p. 221

Beverly is potentially a substantial character. She has feelings and resources; she values loyalty, dedication, diligence, and sensibleness; she is not concerned about her looks. But *Beverly Gray's Problem* is about as close to a moral choice as girl sleuths get. A lovely girl named True Torston is, underneath, a jewel thief. The problem seems a paradox because how could a girl be lovely and likable and yet be a sneak thief?

> Stubbornly her mind clung to the fact that True was the logical suspect. Yet how could she distrust someone she liked. She didn't understand it—but there it was.
>
> *Beverly Gray's Problem*, p. 148

Beverly's suspicions justify a quick snoop into the girl's room. True, as it turns out, is the thief, but only because she is lonely; she learns friendship from Beverly and instantly reforms. In an unusual act for a girl sleuth in pursuit of justice, Beverly doesn't dutifully call the police, but trusts True, and the thief escapes punishment. Friendship works. True turns over a new leaf.

Beverly Gray books contain splurges of the kind of gushy writing that went out with the Outdoor Girls, the kind of prose the syndicate writers gradually abolished. But this is a real writer talking, trying to express profound emotion in a children's book in the 1930s:

> They would remember the modern China and dream about the old China. Wherever they went the native city would be remembered the longest. The narrow streets with dimly lighted shops; the clop-clop of the coolies' shoes as they ran pulling their rickshas; the scent of incense in the little temples and the sound of the temple bells ringing would always be there in their mind's eye to be conjured up at will. They might become famous, they might secure great possessions; yet fame could fade and any possession might be lost, but the memories they gained through their travel could never be taken away. Nothing could deprive them of the thrills they had known at new scenes.
>
> *Beverly Gray on a Treasure Hunt*, pp. 11-12

Except for occasional lush descriptions of heart and soul and moon and magic, the Beverly Gray books—which were enormously popular—are maddening stories which tell you "and a good time was had by all" without divulging a single detail of the fun. The action of the narrative tumbles headlong. The characters may be having dinner on one page, go out on dates in the next paragraph, hear about a plane crash, set out for the rescue and be back home sipping sodas by the next page. With such rapid sequences, the context is lost: the dominant impression one has of Beverly Gray is that she is a gray, shadowy figure—heroic and diligent, but not quite in the world.

This series, without benefit of the high gloss and organization of the syndicate books, is extremely uneven, weak on plot and unity. It sounds funny, but there is something about the sparseness of the style that makes Stratemeyer Syndicate stories read inoffensively. Although they are cliché-ridden, the absence of other distinguishing stylistic features makes them defy judgment. You can't apply the term "bad writing" except to the content. The series are so carefully styleless that you can't point to bad puns, strained metaphors, overloaded descriptions. There is an absence of language: there is vocabulary, but not language. The Beverly Gray books, however, are melodramatic and clumsily written—because they do try to indulge in thoughts and words. Beverly is vague as a cloud while Nancy Drew and the Bobbsey Twins are like cartoon characters—simply and definitively drawn. In an attempt to create dimension, Clair Blank lags behind the syndicate's power to sustain action, and Beverly doesn't come across as a heroine who is either as real and dynamic as Judy Bolton or as thrillingly ideal as Nancy Drew. However, I think the series was popular because Beverly was one of the most adventurous and independent of the girl detectives.

Helen Wells's famous Cherry Ames and Vicki Barr books were more polished. There is a modicum of individuality in these two series (some volumes of which were written by Julie Tatham, who is the same person as Julie Campbell, Trixie Belden's author), but the influence of the successful formula is strong. As nurse and airline hostess, Cherry and Vicki are two career queens who solve mysteries on the job. Nursing was a saleable image in the 1930s and 1940s, and Helen Dore Boyleston made nurse Sue Barton into a household mannikin. Sue Barton was out after a husband, though, and she didn't have time to solve mysteries. By the fourth volume she had married a doctor. Helen Wells, a writer with literary aspirations, was asked to do a series for Grosset & Dunlap, which was looking for a better quality of writing than the anonymous flat-fee writers provided. As a result, she created Cherry Ames, one of the most popular career girls in fiction. Cherry was the nurse I read and loved, and her sleuthing adventures took priority over romance with young interns.

Cherry Ames books have sold more than 5 million copies since the series began during World War II. At one time they were bringing their author $20,000 a year. The first few books were not mysteries but patriotic exaltations of the nursing profession, an inspiration to girls to learn that they were needed. War made it possible.

> As the war deepened, and there were more and greater
> battles, more and still more nurses were going to be needed
> . . . if thousands of men were to be healed and returned to
> battle . . . *if we were to win*. Cherry wished she could cry
> out to other girls, and her voice carry beyond this crowded
> pitiful room, far across the Caribbean and all over the
> United States, how desperately nurses were needed.
>
> *Cherry Ames, Army Nurse*, pp. 192-193

Cherry goes off to war, thrilled and frightened, but in 1944 war was adventure. (Louisa May Alcott became a nurse because it was the only way a woman could get to the war.) If it were not for her secure home in Hilton, Illinois, Cherry's far-flung wanderings might be disturbing to the reader. Home is a little victory garden waiting out the war. Before she leaves to join the army, she takes a sober look at her "own gay little room."

She turned from the window and sat down a moment on the bed. It wore a cherry-red satin cover, with matching covers for her bed pillows, to make it a couch. The small bookshelves at its either end, against the white wall, the twin crystal lamps, the dressing table with its crisp white skirts, and the billowing white curtains tied with wide cherry-red ribbons—all these tempted her to stay. But Cherry could no more have stayed put, doing nothing, than she could have contentedly slept her life away. Her room would be waiting for her, in the exciting meantime.

Cherry Ames, Army Nurse, pp. 14-15

Those white curtains and red bedspread return in volume after volume. By the 1950s and 1960s, when the patriotic style had lost its fervor, readers were made to forget that Cherry had ever been to war, lest she turn into a middle-aged spinster. Moreover, the glamour of nursing itself could not be sustained, and very soon Cherry was playing detective. Helen Wells says, "My two series were primarily mystery stories because this is what Grosset & Dunlap wanted. A market existed, and still exists, for juvenile mysteries. The reason is as crass as that." But she finds the relationship between reader and author an intimate one. "It's like writing in a straitjacket—or on a tiny canvas with only three colors to work with. Yet within this tiny scope one can try to be honest, to be fun, to project real feeling, honest observations, values one believes in. Literary values? The series have none. Entertainment values, yes."[1]

Cherry Ames is only accidentally effectual as a sleuth—because she is a nurse, extremely efficient, with an observant eye and cool head, she solves messy situations with as much flair as she makes beds with hospital corners. Cherry's mysteries rarely require the courage and action of Nancy Drew. Instead, their appeal is the glamour and romance associated with the independent, hard-working, fancy-free, free-wheeling career girl. She's sharp and chic, though little attention is paid to her looks. Except for a few occasions, when Cherry is admired by her patients and superiors, she is almost sexless. Her charm is simple.

> Cherry was shining proof that beauty and brains went together. Cherry's dark-brown, almost black eyes, black curly hair, and red cheeks, which had won her the name of Cherry, always called forth admiring remarks. Her patients appreciated her cheerful presence.
>
> The doctors and head nurses recognized Cherry's ability and skill as a nurse and her deep interest in nursing. She could use her head when clear thinking was needed. And she was as good as a detective about getting the facts of anything.
>
> *Cherry Ames, Island Nurse,* p. 3

Cherry doesn't use her sex to buy approval. She is never flirtatious. She is almost above romance, though it occurs regularly, and she is without commitment. The elusive young doctors who parade through the stories leave the impression that romance is so easily available that there is no need to snatch at the future. Cherry will bide her time.

On the other hand, Cherry's sex inhibits her. She is forever afraid that she hasn't enough expertise or experience to assist the new Dr. Kildare on the case. Although she can do *simple* lab tests in an emergency, she believes that "any nurse who tries to play doctor isn't a very responsible nurse." (*Cherry Ames, Department Store Nurse*, p. 14) On an amnesia case, she assists a psychiatrist and frantically looks back to her one psychology course in nursing school. She discovers that there can be sickness of the mind as well as of the body. She is cautious with the amnesia patient.

Talking, or forcing Bob to talk, could be as disastrous as giving a patient the wrong medicine. Better wait for Dr. Hope to lead the way.

The Case of the Forgetful Patient, p. 17

Dr. Hope! And *he* chooses Cherry! ("It surprised her to have this doctor turn to her informally and ask her opinion," p. 28)

Cherry's real ace is her efficiency, the prime quality of a nurse. Her nursing ability is "feminine"—maternal, soothing, caring. It is glorified diaper changing, an essential service. Cherry's visiting nurse's bag is full of clues to her competence. It is a miniature hospital with delightful compartments of medicines and swabs and needles and tubing: the old Honey Bunch nest. Because she is so neat and good at holding hands, Cherry's confidence has improved through the years. The early books dramatize her fear of failure. She frequently is in trouble before the authorities—the hospital or the military. In the later books, as she turns toward sleuthing, she becomes more confident.

Cherry Ames's airborne counterpart is Vicki Barr, one of a host of female fliers—Ruth Darrow, Dorothy Dix, the Girl Aviators, and the Flying Girl, among others. Practically as soon as Orville and Wilbur had gotten off the ground, the Flying Girl was flapping her wings. The Vicki Barr series, however, oozes glamour out of being an airline hostess, a step-and-fetch-it for passengers and pilots. Most girl sleuths can fly solo if necessary, and Vicki can tinker with an airplane engine and pilots a Piper Cub in *Peril over the Airport*, but one assumes she will never fly for TWA—although she hopes "the time would come when women would be at the controls on the flight deck." (*The Mystery of Flight 508*, p. 104)

Vicki Barr is a tenacious, independent-minded young woman who has a cheerleader's flair for friendliness, but her major interest is solving mysteries, which seem to occur regularly on her flights. She craves adventure and she is a tough sleuth. She is flattered by admiring talk, but she won't stand for male gossip about helpless females. She solves an FBI case on her first hostess run.

> Yet no one could have appeared less adventurous than Vicki Barr. She was small, with a delicate, almost shy, face, and soft ash-blonde hair. She seemed very fragile. But the fragility belied strong, wiry muscles and an amazing capacity for beefsteak. The dreaminess, if you looked closely, was more intentness, the absorbed look of a girl busy thinking up action—or mischief.
>
> Her airy grace, the smallness and blondeness of her, made Vicki seem about as durable as a cream puff. Actually, she was as sturdy as a young tree.
>
> *Silver Wings for Vicki,* pp. 1-2

Vicki is shrewd, though romantic, delicate but tough. She likes to wear perfume and high heels and flowing dresses. She is proud of her blue uniform. The description of her reveals a deep paradox in the career girl sleuth books: it is deeply "feminine" to have an "appearance" and to seem what you are not. It is also a surprise to be other than you seem—to have brains as well as prettiness, toughness as well as fragility, to be human and also female, to have actual muscles as well as a fairylike fragility. Girls can identify with being small-dainty-feminine-inferior, and yet they can be up there with the boys—tough and untouchable, worldly and free.

Flying, more than any dream of man-womankind, means freedom, and for a girl to be an airline stewardess is the height of bliss. As Vicki goes to sleep the night she arrives in glowing New York to go to airline school, after her first flight, she falls into dream-ecstasy:

The silver plane—the clouds—the night sky—the girl in blue—what a voyage it had been. And now this tall, brilliant city—why, the very reflections in the window shimmered like—shimmered like—diamonds and like silver planes—like silver—like—

Silver Wings for Vicki, p. 49

Major sources of my illusions about New York are right there in the first two Vicki Barr books. The scene is as glittering and golden as Gatsby's mansion—the table "gleaming with white damask and silver and crystal"; "ice skaters in white plumes, and waterfalls and crystal chandeliers." (*Vicki Finds the Answer*, p. 29) Vicki is fascinated "by the whole tinkling, softly sparkling room." "It's so lavish—there's so much of New York!" (P. 24)

Vicki is romantic, but romance with men is sketchy. The leading male interest, pilot Dean Fletcher, is stand-offish and chauvinistic about women in general, and the romance hardly gets off the ground—though there are a few cautious kisses. Vicki is servant to her pilots, bringing them coffee and cheer when the storms and air pockets come. "Captain Jordan was a hearty, comfortable, dependable man, one of the nicest of the 'big brother' pilots." (*Vicki Finds the Answer*, p. 32)

The assumption is that Vicki's daddy wouldn't let her go gallivanting off into the blue unless there was such a comfortable male to take care of her. Such is innocence.

Of course a flying girl sleuth could not be so carefree, so eager to whirl into the blue sky unless, like Cherry Ames, she had a home to come back to. When she isn't on global glamour duty for Federal Airlines, Vicki lives in "the Castle"—a large old house with a tower (in Illinois)—with her family.

> The Castle—though not very large—had a tower, high
> Norman-casement windows, sloping red-tiled roof, an
> upstairs balcony, a buttressed oak entrance door. The
> grounds, too, resembled the park of a castle: a sweeping
> lawn setting the house well back off the road, spreading
> shade trees, a rock garden, a rose and peony garden, stone
> birdbaths and benches. Behind the house apple and cherry
> trees grew. Then the grassy hill rolled downward, became a
> little wood, and led steeply down to the lake.
>
> *Silver Wings for Vicki*, pp. 11-12

Vicki's young, pretty mom is a skilled horsewoman and
her crazy professor father is a Sunday chef. With
Freckles the dog and freckled Ginny, the sister in
braces, they are the staples of a Midwest home-base
which is lovingly lingered over for a spell in each book, a
lull of security in the midst of high and mighty
adventures in the sky. They let the little reader scared to
death of flying (me) know that the girl detective always
has a haven of safety. Vicki is an Amelia Earhart who
always comes home. Typical of the stereotype that
fathers are protective and oppressive, and mothers are
indulgent and frustrated, Vicki's father very nearly locks
her up in the Castle tower to keep her from going up in
an airplane, but Vicki's mother wishes she could go to
airline school too.

The books are about home, really. In our civilization
the female idea of adventure is to set up a home
wherever you go. Besides the Castle, Vicki has her safe
New York apartment and her snug airship.

> Vicki always felt like a hostess when she was on duty.
> The comfortable, up-to-date ship was her air-borne apart-
> ment, and the little galley in the back, her kichenette.
>
> *Behind the White Veil*, p. 2

No Barr book is complete without Vicki preparing meals for her passengers in that little kitchenette. Food is sumptuous. Vicki eats exotic dishes wherever she goes (pralines and gumbo and jambalaya in New Orleans, for instance). If she were still flying, she would be presiding over the Chicken Chow Mein Flight and the Luau of the Skies.

Every time I fly, the flock of hostesses hastening up the aisles causes Vicki Barr to surface like a reflex in my memory. I deeply suspect Vicki Barr resides in the subconsciouses of at least half of those glamour girls who are not always so pretty and innocent as you think hostesses are supposed to be if you grew up on *Silver Wings for Vicki*.

The glamour girl image is even more extravagant in Connie Blair mysteries, the most obviously sexist and the least inspiring of them all. While there may be some harmless escapism in girls' mysteries (and any mystery fiction), I have the impression that the priority of Connie Blair books (by Betsy Allen) is sexist teachings. Connie Blair works at an advertising agency and her job is somehow supposed to be rewarding and thrilling.

> . . . in that busy agency girls, to be popular, kept their minds on their jobs.
>
> *Puzzle in Purple*, p. 84

Connie works her way up to copywriter at Reid & Renshaw. She carries out important assignments in Mexico and Bermuda and Philadelphia. Connie Blair mysteries are colors (*Riddle in Red, Clue in Blue*, etc.) because Connie likes colors—as an advertising schemer she has an eye for color, less for its aesthetic than its commercial value. The series glamorizes the charisma of the advertising world.

She felt that . . . she had failed in a time of emergency. An inward monitor made her want to redeem herself, made her long for the satisfaction of being able to search out the culprit and deliver the precious mink back into the furrier's hands.

The Yellow Warning, p. 111

The series stresses appearance, popularity, and feminity as I.D. cards for entry into the business world. Connie uses her sex consciously—to gain approval, to gain information, to get a promotion.

She put a hand on his arm and looked at him in a way that would have melted a stronger man.

The Yellow Warning, p. 123

(Nancy Drew doesn't stoop so low.)

She tried to look especially appealing and demure, because she wanted to get her information in a hurry.

The Silver Secret, p. 64

In Philadelphia Connie's beaus help her solve her cases and they take her to classy restaurants.

The Yellow Warning (1951), with singular tastelessness, shows Connie devising a plan to advertise furs with photographs of models at the zoo: a girl in a lynx coat admiring the lynxes, a girl in a fox coat standing by the fox cage, and a gorilla in his own coat wistfully admiring a model. This cheap horror underscores the basic values of the series: exploitation and appearances. Connie feels responsible to a big business furrier when a valuable mink disappears. She thinks she is his servant.

> Connie knew, as she buttered her roll without glancing up, that Andy was looking at her appreciatively. It made her feel warm and attractive.
>
> *The Yellow Warning*, p. 87

In the early books Connie can't go out the door without the reader being told how she looks that day. She is neat, chic, blonde. Even when she loses sleep over a case, she doesn't lose her looks.

> There were dark circles under Connie's eyes, making them look large and compassionate.
>
> *The Yellow Warning*, p. 100

Other girl sleuths are outside time and history—they are mythic—but Connie Blair mysteries are concerned with immediate commercial and social values. The stories have a certain psychological dimension, but the effect is flat and flabby. The later stories conform more rigidly to the conventional girl detective formula, and Connie gains more freedom.

Betsy Allen, the author of the series, is a pseudonym for Betty Cavanna, whose melodramatic books for adolescents and teenage girls are highly recommended by the reviewers and librarians who disdain series books—who would burn the Bobbseys if they got a chance. Learning about their approval of Cavanna's fiction, I am dubious about their judgment—and those of parents and teachers and everyone else except children themselves—when it comes to deciding what children should read. Some critics dismiss Nancy Drews as trash and say they should be taken away—like comics and cigarettes—if children are caught with them. Cecile Megaliff, in *The Junior Novel*, discounts the series books as simple-minded, but says that Betty Cavanna's novels have been highly recommended for their realistic attention to topics girls are interested in and for their positive values.[2] Megaliff notes that "no adverse criticisms of her choice of topics has been made." Yet here are Cavanna's topics:

> The situations are those which would appeal to girls. Diane accepts class rings from two boys. Jody tries to adjust herself to unfamiliar surroundings and ways of life in a foreign school. Andrea tries to sail a boat by herself when she is not ready to do so and has to be rescued by the hero. The same situation occurs when Sue Scott tries to jump hurdles when she is not ready to do so. Deborah Sanford tries to save money to be able to go to a very special weekend party with Craig. . . .
>
> *The Junior Novel*, pp. 29-30

The sentiment of these stories—which have titles such as *Boy Next Door*, *A Girl Can Dream*, *Paintbox Summer*, *Passport to Romance*, and *Going on Sixteen*—is not far removed from that in the Connie Blair series. Some of Cavanna's stories are for pubescents and some for teenagers, graduates from sleuth stories.

> Miss Cavanna does not write literary masterpieces, but she has much to offer adolescents. . . . Her characters are not wild, flighty creatures far removed from reality. They are interested in school, clothes, and boys, which are the things that do concern the average teen-age girl.
>
> *The Junior Novel*, p. 31

The Junior Novel recommends Betty Cavanna's works and similar books by such authors as Anne Emory and Mary Stolz as the answer for girls who are especially frightened about growing up and leaving home and getting married. A review is quoted: "A good choice for any girl who is beginning to think of the years ahead." (P. 37) Betty Cavanna deals with "teenage girl problems

ranging from brother adoration to high heels." (P. 36)
Mary Stolz's books on the problems of teenage marriage
are praised: "Betty Wilder, when she falls in love,
realizes why her mother is content to be a housewife."
(P. 69)

And what about a girl's other longings?—her need for
adventure, her desire to do things and solve problems,
her interest in the world? If these junior novels were the
only choice besides the series books, I would promote
Nancy Drew and Judy Bolton to the ends of the earth.
The series books for pubescent girls share the
externalized focus of the boys' books—adventurous,
outgoing, wide open to the world—although they return
to a cozy symbolic nest. But the junior novels the reader
graduates to are thoroughly internalized. They promote
characters who are fretful and thoughtful, troubled
about their identity. These teenagers (without career
aspirations) worry all the time about being accepted.
(The newer stories, following the trends of the romance
magazines, are about realistic problems such as family
squabbles and unwanted pregnancies. The new heroines
aren't always pretty or perfect.) It would seem that the
eleven-year-old, sexually immature reader of Nancy
Drew is allowed more freedom to explore the outside
world than the teenage girl who is more definitely
trapped by her sex role.

I tried reading some "junior miss" novels recently to
see if they could sustain my interest as dozens of
mystery books obviously have during the writing of
these chapters. But they bored and annoyed me. I can
still at my age zip through a Nancy Drew with fondness
and feel that my imagination is freed in a special way.
The story is so lean that the imagination is forced to
supply the settings and details. In the series books I see
the sources of my dreams, while in the junior novels I

see the conventional female role against which I rebelled, from the beginning. Perhaps the ways I resisted it, and the ways my own imagination was directed by the series books, are revealed in a fragment of one of my own pieces of writing from age eleven.

Writing is the closest you can come to being a girl detective in real life at that age. I wrote the Carson Girls series, and I still have *The Carson Girls Go Abroad*. A glance at my little mystery story reveals no child prodigy, no creative imagination blossoming, only a frustrated but nevertheless determined child who was busily resisting the Honey Bunch/Junior Miss model. My little story reveals a desperate dependence on escapist fantasies. It was an amalgamation of Nancy Drew, the Danas, the Bobbseys, Vicki Barr, and Cherry Ames. I couldn't even think of an original name for my girls. I took it simply from Nancy Drew's father, Carson Drew.

The Carson Girls Go Abroad was about twins, Sue and Jean, whose father was a famous detective and whose mother was significantly nonexistent. The girls had a modest flair for solving mysteries. Jean was the serious, practical twin—grimly mature and already latched to a boyfriend. Sue, the more adventurous, tomboyish twin (a thin projection of myself), was resentful of her sister's boyfriend and had no plans to marry. She wanted to be an airline hostess and she bought a book, *How to Become a Stewardess in Five Easy Lessons*. Jean planned to be a nurse: she was more feminine, good at making beds and fixing food. As the book opened they were choosing their careers and celebrating their eighteenth birthdays with a surprise party (with ice cream, dainty sandwiches, pickles, candies, puddings, cakes, and pies) and a trip to the State Fair in Louisville (with cotton candy and candied apples and lemonade) where Sue had a narrow escape from the Snake Woman. Nothing happened to Jean, who was protected by her boyfriend.

The mystery was about a stolen stamp collection (the fictional version of my own dime-store album). A prominent citizen had his valuable collection stolen but it was mysteriously returned the next day. Then the Carson Girls heard a burglar in their own house and soon afterward discovered that one of their stamps, an odd Romanian portrait of a bespectacled man whose hairline was askew, had faded. The Carson Girls, according to the newspaper, theorized that a ring of counterfeiters was operating in the vicinity, "borrowing" stamp collections and making copies of valuable stamps.

In the meantime, the Carson Twins went on a trip to France with their father and their French maid, Mlle. Bleax (my conception of a French name). Jean's boyfriend piloted his own private plane across the ocean and Sue played air hostess. Jean wore a helmet and goggles and sat in the cockpit with her boyfriend and also played ship's nurse. When they got to France, they toured the provinces and saw the famous Percheron horses Sue had read about in geography. While they were in France, they became curious about a stamp shop and soon became involved in a fascinating set of adventures. As it turned out, the counterfeiting ring was operating right there in provincial France, and the Carson girls solved the mystery, mainly because of Sue's daring and logical mind. Jean was too busy with her boyfriend to contribute much. The twins won a fabulous reward for catching the crooks, and with the reward they would be able to go to airline hostess and nursing school.

It bothered me that Nancy Drew never accepted rewards. She solved mysteries for the fun of it. If pressed, she would accept a token—an ivory charm, an old clock, a locket, all souvenirs for a hope chest. The Hardy Boys, on the other hand, were building up a bank account for their future career. They went out after rewards and they got them.

When I went to New York to pursue a career, my life would have been a perfectly circular pattern had I ended up as a junior editor on a juvenile mystery syndicate, cranking out the very dreams that led me there in the first place. As it was I did the next most obvious thing: I wrote for the fan magazines. And through them I discovered the essence of the girl detective. The TV and movie fan mags have an effect on the emotions similar to that of the girl sleuths and Bobbsey books—but they are sleazy, calculated, and faddish. I have no doubt that Harriet S. Adams, the author of Nancy Drew, is sincerely concerned with contributing to a child's emotional welfare. She has commented that serious children's books on social problems are "completely uncalled for and unwholesome" and are published "just to make a fast dollar." She protests, "Why make children all weeping and worried? Children's reading should be pleasant and lighthearted."[3] The fan magazines, however, have no self-redeeming streak, and the easy morals they preach are calculated to captivate two groups: women and teenie-boppers. The women they write for are either bored housewives or desperate outcasts who wish they were housewives. These women read the Liz Taylor scandals with immense satisfaction, feeling superior to Taylor (Liz can't bear children) and at the same time helplessly entranced by wealth, status, and glamour. The magazines congratulate the readers on their domesticity, while titillating them with the escapades of "immoral" or victimized Beautiful Souls.

The other sort of fan magazine story attracts adolescent girls who avidly read about the Dr. Kildare or David Cassidy of the moment. The fan desires proof that the star is "just like me" (moral, straight, friendly), but is excited by the taboo world which cloaks the idol. She is jealous and envious—even hateful—and she is downright destroyed if her favorite does something evil which threatens the heavens to fall. I know that hundreds of little girls panicked when Mike Landon of *Bonanza* divorced. Some threatened suicide.

Here are two ends of a spectrum of exploitation: the girl who is sold the dream and the grown woman she turns out to be. Both the fan mags and the girl sleuth books alienate women from themselves—the dreams and romance sweetly entrancing, intensifying the little girl/ housewife's dissatisfaction with herself and her environment, blinding her to healthful possibilities, reinforcing values which close off experimentation and imagination. Given this schizophrenia, there is no regular and full way to become an imaginative, mature woman.

The girl sleuth is the supreme role given to females in juvenile fiction, the role which allows more freedom than any particular career. The girl wins approval and achieves success through her sleuthing more than through her job. Detecting allows her to use her brains. Cherry and Vicki just adore their work, yet they are only assistants to men with more important tasks. The fringe benefits of dedicated service are exotic places, fascinating people, puzzles, footprints, and clues. Thus, the books subscribe to a male view of the world. The career books glamorize the standard daintiness, docility, and dullness of femininity by officially admitting girls into the outside world and rewarding them for what is after all only glorified maid service. A girl has to resort to snooping in order to make use of her talents.

The girl sleuth, a product of the stirrings of liberation, is potentially a pathfinder and an explorer. But, unfortunately, she has been on the same path for a hundred years. It was Louisa May Alcott, really, who opened up the frontier for the career girl heroine when she published *Little Women* in 1861. Alcott was my first feminist heroine and perhaps it is axiomatic in the life of the American girl that *Little Women* is equal in influence to Nancy Drew. In spite of its obvious sentimentality, it is popular because Alcott was a superb storyteller and champion of feminist individualism. She was highly imaginative and in a constant fret about the social restrictions placed on girls. "I was born with a boy's spirit under my bib and tucker," she wrote in her journal.[4] And when asked to write a column of advice for young women, she responded with sketches of her spinster heroines and titled them "Happy Women." But Alcott was a commercial writer who happily reflected many values of the times. She wrote several series, as well as a couple of "dime novel" mysteries. I believe none of the popular writers of subsequent series have equaled her vigor and style and her insistence on feminist rights. None of them improved on her story-telling ability, and except for getting them behind the wheel and into jeans, none of them have surpassed her vision of freedom for women. Alcott, writing for a popular market, did not always carry through this vision. It is interesting that she set a precedent for imprisonment as well as for liberation: she never intended to let her heroine, Jo March, who was modeled on herself, marry and settle down. But after Part I of *Little Women* was so favorably received, her public and publisher pressured her into inventing a husband for Jo.

Women writers of popular literature have hardly escaped that fundamental assumption—that the goal of life for a girl is a happy marriage. They have indulged instead in prolonging the state of girlhood. The series form provides timelessness, and the heroine is a perpetual girl, free to entertain the possibility of an alternative identity to conventional womanhood. In early series books, characters such as Pollyanna and Elsie Dinsmore grew up and married and even experienced widowhood; the series of the twentieth century contrived to sell the image of liberation by keeping the heroines at a stage where they had relative freedom.

The girl sleuth, a transitional heroine, has been influential, but there is a need now for a heroine in juvenile fiction who can find fulfillment in diverse ways. The mystery-adventure form, which can be splendid and captivating as entertainment, can accomodate heroines of more substance and diversity, with more dignity and personal style than the glamour girls or the standard-ized, updated Nancy Drews.

7

Impostor Tea

Nancy Drew and her shadows, the Dana Girls, are the only major girl detectives left in print now that Cherry Ames, Judy Bolton, and Connie Blair are being phased out. Nancy's popularity is increasing, owing to a new publicity push which includes a "Haunted House Merchandiser"—a bookstore display of Stratemeyer sleuths. Grosset & Dunlap, deciding that it has been tapping only 5 percent of the juvenile market, has plans to triple the series' sales within four or five years.[1] The entire Nancy Drew series is still on the shelves—in classy new covers with changing texts to match the times.

I just sent off four Raisin Bran proof-of-purchase seals for a free copy of *The Secret of Mirror Bay*, one of the newer Nancy Drew mysteries. When I got it, I noticed some of the things Nancy and her friends were eating.

> The appetizing dish turned out to be cheese soufflé served with tiny ham sandwiches, corn on the cob, and tomato salad.
>
> *The Secret of Mirror Bay*, p. 59

Then came dessert.

It proved to be a generous helping of wild strawberry
mousse heaped in the center of a ring of fluffy sponge cake.
The Secret of Mirror Bay, p. 67

Nancy always dined sumptuously of course, but the
new books are sweeter and starchier; perhaps the
attractive food is a luscious sex substitute. I don't know
if my Nancy-fed fantasies made hoeing beans or picking
blackberries more or less bearable when I was eleven,
but I do know I was turned on by the delightful
daintiness and regularity of Nancy's repasts. Mrs. Gruen
served homemade delectables for midnight snacks.
Picnics were rapturous outings with old-fashioned
hampers and checkered "luncheon cloths" spread in a
mossy glade—no bugs and no litter and no noisy
neighboring picnickers. No problems except assailants
and spies lurking in the bushes. To this day I cherish
somewhere in my memory an imagined perfect picnic,
with a real wicker picnic hamper and a checkered
luncheon cloth groaning with glorious delicacies.

The current editions of Nancy Drew mysteries
continue to thrive on tea-party coziness.

"Good afternoon," Nancy said. "We'd like to have some
tea and cinnamon toast, and stay here until the storm dies
down."
The Sign of the Twisted Candles, p. 5

And when she returns home from her adventure, the
same thrill awaits:

Nancy said, "Let's all go into the living room and
exchange stories. Dad, build a nice cozy fire, will you? It's
chilly."

Nancy, her friends and family can stop and enjoy food at a tearoom or discuss a mystery over a midnight snack—a "feminine" pleasure denied male characters such as the Hardy Boys. Frank and Joe Hardy, aged fifteen and sixteen, zip through their mysteries as fast as little kids wearing out their blue jeans. In the Hardy Boys series (also a Stratemeyer production), eating is just stopping for gas. (In fact, they have a mother precisely because someone has to do the cooking.) Even in the "grown-up" Lew Archer mysteries by Ross Macdonald, Archer grabs a sandwich at a lunch counter, anxious to get on with the case, though he may pause to flirt with the waitress. Meals are an automatic service the boys seem entitled to during pit stops from the chase. But Nancy Drew is never in such a hurry on an overnight crook chase that she doesn't have time to pack a neat little bag with p.j.'s and perfume and panties. Bess brings along extra food.

Along with the renewed emphasis on food in the Stratemeyer series books, comes a 1973 surprise, a supplement to Nancy's sleuthing. It's the *Nancy Drew Cookbook: Clues to Good Cooking*. (Nancy Drew, she's incredible!) Cherry Ames has her own nursing handbook; the Hardy Boys have a detective handbook (with the latest crime detection methods—bugging and so forth); and the Bobbsey Twins have their own guide to the care and keeping of the flag—an appendix at the end of their *Red, White and Blue Mystery*. So it was inevitable that Nancy should issue her own guidebook.

But why a cookbook? Why, at a time when Nancy's skills should have broadened to include mechanics, computer programming, electronic counter-surveillance, and space travel—why a cookbook? Harriet S. Adams says, "The popularity of cookbooks was the determining factor for Nancy Drew to create *Clues to Good Cooking*."[2] Yet I might have expected *Nancy's Guide to Sports* or *Nancy's Guide to Self-Reliance* or some ecological handbook. Or, better, a *Guide to Sleuthing* from this wonder-girl gumshoe with the magnifying glass eternally poised over a footprint. In fact, there *are* plans for a Nancy Drew book on sleuthing, according to her author. But the cooking comes first.

> Nancy enjoys buying unusual glass or crockery containers in which to pour her apple butter. She sometimes uses empty jelly, peanut butter, or pickle jars and decorates them with seals to fit the holiday or celebration.
> *Nancy Drew Cookbook*, p. 153

And:

> Nancy finds that half an orange slice and a sprig of mint or a green cherry for every cupful makes a pretty decoration and a tasty one, too!
> *Nancy Drew Cookbook*, p. 71

If the cookbook had come out when I was twelve, I would have felt horribly betrayed. Now I feel it confirms my assessment of the series and provides a convenient postscript. This is what Nancy is *really* all about. Here is proof of the pudding, so to speak, for Nancy is liberated from the kitchen but she hasn't abandoned it. Actually, contemporary Nancy Drew is no slave to a stove. Most of her recipes are modern short-cut quick-mix cop-outs. She makes flake pastry by buying frozen patty shells and flattening them with a rolling pin. (Julia Child spends the livelong day on croissants.) Nancy's homemade apple butter is spiced-up store-bought apple sauce. The cookbook throws in a little nature food faddism, with wheat germ and honey in a few recipes. Nancy dollops blackstrap molasses on her cornbread, not knowing the difference between blackstrap and sorghum. (Blackstrap is wicked stuff.) Nancy bakes a cake just to show off her talents, but Ruth Fielding, one of her predecessors in fiction, churned butter out of necessity. Cooking, for Nancy, is just for fun, and she behaves according to all the pop-top jiffy-flap/patio barbecue/TV dinner/cookout norms. Even the boys share a role: Mr. Drew contributes his surprise specialty—cheesecake in a springform pan! If the sex roles are going to be violated, it is not a serious matter, just all-American fun. Nancy might have instructed us in judo and karate. Instead her cookbook underscores the same old line of the series: Nancy digs being dainty, and domesticity is, after all, still where it's at for a girl. The *Nancy Drew Cookbook*, however unwittingly, affirms Nancy's eternal femininity.

The cookbook is two-thirds the length and twice the price of a regular book in the series. The fancy cover is a photograph of an elegant dining table with candlelight and flowers and donuts and muffins and ham and milk in wine glasses. In the shadowy background there appears to be the rear view of a man. The recipes take their names from titles in the series: how fantastic! "The Mystery of the 99 Steps" is not a weird architectural puzzle but a recipe for French toast! "The Invisible Intruder" is only out after a midnight snack ("Invisible Intruder's Coconut Custard"). "The Message in the Hollow Oak" is a recipe for Hollow Oak Nest Eggs. In a little mystery à la carte, Nancy finds a missing heirloom ring in the blueberry muffins. She also makes "Impostor Tea," "Crumbling Wall Coffee Cake," "Dancing Puppet Parfait," "Sleuth Soup," and "Vanishing Nut Bread." Nancy fans, it seems, would rather gobble Detective Burgers than examine the parsley in the butter, as Sherlock Holmes did.

According to Nancy's prolific author, Stratemeyer Syndicate has been concerned with revising its books to suit today's readers. "Adoption laws, for example, have been instituted since many of our stories first appeared on the market. Modes of travel have changed, too, so we have replaced the trains of earlier editions with planes."[3] Nancy's new world is a cosmopolitan global village with jet-linked suburbs and African safaris on zebra-striped tourist buses. Nancy flies around as conveniently as a business executive, and she takes a private helicopter when she needs to get to the boondocks in a hurry. She still carries her flashlight everywhere and attends Sunday church services without fail. But now she wears jeans and "pants suits," rumples her hair thoughtfully, drinks Coke, and watches TV. Her convertible has air conditioning. Some new words have broken through the icy dialogue—"neat," "weird," "groovy," and "icky."

Although Nancy's environment has enlarged, and there is an attempt to accommodate changing social values, Nancy has not yet come truly down to earth. In the revised *Message in the Hollow Oak*, Nancy goes to Cairo, Illinois, on the Ohio River, on an archaeological expedition. Cairo is not far from my childhood home and I remember its reputation as a rough river town full of gamblers and whores. But when Nancy and her friends go there, they find the old tea-party scene.

Together the eight visitors strolled around the small town. Many of the houses were modest frame structures, but on a lovely tree-lined street they found several Victorian mansions.

One stately red-brick house was open for inspection and they took the tour. As they walked through the handsome high-ceilinged rooms . . . .

The Message in the Hollow Oak, p. 95

However, Nancy *has* changed, though she still sees through special lenses. Much of the old snobbery has disappeared. Harriet S. Adams says, "To me Nancy Drew is the ideal, all-American girl who is modern but not ultra-modern, helpful to people of all ages and from all countries. She is not prejudiced against people of any race, color, or creed, but works hard to uncover evildoers and bring them to justice. I assume from the popularity of these books that this is truly what today's juvenile readers want to read and, therefore, I am proud to be writing this type of story."[4]

The racism and snobbery which were an inherent part of the original series—because they were an inherent part of the society it mirrored—have been dealt with firmly in the revisions and newer volumes. There is a healthy new attitude toward class distinctions. Hannah Gruen, for instance, has been granted personhood: she now has friends and feelings and interests. She is a walking encyclopedia of ornithology, her hobby. The new *Clue in the Jewel Box* erases the remark about the exiled queen's suspicious foreign accent, although the plot about the impostor prince and the royal jewels remains. In *The Double Jinx Mystery* a suspicious foreign girl with an olive complexion turns out to be a friend.

Kammy did not look at the girls unpleasantly but she did not smile either. The slightly dark shadows under her eyes gave the Eurasian young woman a rather mysterious, troubled expression.

The Double Jinx Mystery, p. 21

Crooks are the same old breed, still associated with the powers of darkness:

> He was middle-aged and had a swarthy complexion. His dark hair was long and he wore a full beard. De Keer's outstanding feature were his black eyes which glistened intensely.
>
> "He may be talented," Nancy thought, "but I'll bet he's cruel and scheming."

The Whispering Statue, rev. ed., pp. 121-122

The Spider Sapphire Mystery (1968) seems bent on atoning for the series' past racism. It introduces Black Africans in a sympathetic light, although the mystery concerns, as usual, the precious property of aristocrats. In that story Nancy goes to Africa to search for a missing man ("a fine-looking black") falsely accused of stealing the priceless spider sapphire. Other good Blacks appear, including a lovely singer, Madame Lilia Bulawaya, who sings "several delightful songs in Swahili. . . . Not only was her voice sweet but she had a charming personality." (P. 47) (However, the British guide of Nancy's safari is called affectionately "our White Hunter." [P. 74]) The evil of a renegade African Black named Swahili Joe is explained by an injury which left him "uncoordinated" and thus not responsible for carrying out the orders of a jewel thief gang. The conspirators are suspicious swarthies from India, but the jewel belongs to a good Indian.

Except for the Africans, black characters have been largely kept out of the series. *The Secret of Mirror Bay* attempts at least a reference to social consciousness.

Nancy and her friends visit the Baseball Hall of Fame, where Ned admires Babe Ruth, but Nancy prefers Leroy Satchel Paige, because he once said, "Don't look back—something might be gaining on you."

> The others agreed this was great advice, not only in a baseball game, but also in life.
>
> *The Secret of Mirror Bay*, p. 141

The saying certainly applies to the Nancy Drew series: Nancy can't afford to look back.

In spite of her progress in the new series, Nancy confronts the same dilemma: she works on a mystery and some men try to stop her. They are more frequently termed Nancy's "enemies," so it is clearer that they are out to get her. Her predicaments and injuries continue. In *The Double Jinx Mystery* she comes down with a bird disease; the crooks have taken to shooting guns at her tires. Harriet Adams points out that the texture of the stories has significantly changed: "Where a plot was old-fashioned, it has been completely rewritten and a sub-plot has been added. In *Nancy Drew: The Invisible Intruder* there are five sub-plots! Today's sophisticated readers enjoy complicated mysteries."[5]

While the mysteries have become more complicated, the characters have been simplified, if that is possible, and their shallowness remains one of the series' greatest problems. Between 1972 and 1973 there were sharp changes in Bess and George, deleting the exaggerated and unfair characterizations of female roles: "feminine" Bess and "tomboy" George. In the 1972 version of *The Message in the Hollow Oak*, Bess is as squeamish as ever. She flees to the kitchen when she is shown some bones dug up from an Indian mound, and she plays Cupid in an unusually long jealousy sub-plot. In *The Secret of*

Mirror Bay, published the same year, Bess is less picky but still weak.

> She was not particularly keen about going on the trek because of the green man, but since her friends were making the climb she felt compelled to go along. Nancy felt no alarm and tried to reassure Bess.
>
> *The Secret of Mirror Bay*, p. 60

However, *The Double Jinx Mystery* (1973) removes Bess's daintiness and George's rough behavior, but without these stereotypes, and with no new dimensions to their characters, they are like balloons slowly losing air.

Bess and George have more to do in the newer books, and so their blandness is spread like mayonnaise through every mystery. Their boyfriends help too.

> Burt was of medium height, husky and blond, while Dave was tall and rangy, with green eyes.
>
> *The Clue of the Broken Locket*, rev. ed., p. 119

That is about the extent of our knowledge of Burt and Dave, though they have major roles, along with college chum Ned Nickerson. Ned is less Nancy's protector now than her friend, and the change is for the better, though Ned still has an important "masculine" function. When Nancy sees a hidden message in a high crevice she calls to "six-foot Ned" to reach it. Six-foot Ned gets to kiss Nancy occasionally these days too. Sometimes Nancy rescues him from peril: in *The Mystery of the Glowing Eye* (1974) it is Ned who is kidnapped. But the trend toward equality has its limits. In that book (one of the few to show Nancy confused and doubtful), she is jealous of a high-handed lawyer who is trying to take not only her mystery but her father away from her.

Marty King ("a twenty-four-year-old platinum blonde") is a good legal assistant, but Mr. Drew is forced to fire her when she asks him to marry her. I suppose this forwardness is supposed to represent female liberation, but the truth is that Nancy and Marty King are competing over who gets to be protected by Carson Drew. The career woman is not portrayed favorably, and both she and Nancy require male protection in order to thrive.

There is a new emphasis on teamwork, and as a result Nancy is less absurdly superior, but also less heroic. She has lost some of her stature as Super-Sleuth, now that she is less snobbish. In the past Nancy was sometimes a smarty pants, and in *The Whispering Statue* and *The Haunted Bridge* she was a prig. Although she is still a strong leader, much of her supremacy in the old days depended on a greater seriousness about her mission to mop up evil—which was more insidious and threatening, apparently, when it rose out of the great heap of n'er-do-wells that crowded the original books. Now her activities—happily rid of many of those damaging stereotypes—are filled with more jovial teenage fun. While the Bobbsey Twins have become more grown-up in recent books, and very serious about solving mysteries, Nancy has become less so. Both series reflect an emerging youth class, privileged by early sophistication and postponed adulthood.

The illustrations of the Nancy Drew series show the evolution of Nancy from an independent career woman to a fluffy kitten child. In the early books Nancy wore suits and hats and gloves and she meant business. She reflected the career woman of the 1930s and 1940s, when ads often pictured women as mature, self-possessed human beings—not crinolined angels, fluffy dumplings, or bleached bikini blondes. R. H. Tandy's famous drawings portrayed a self-possessed young woman with a graceful figure, who sometimes had a smirk on her face as she snooped behind a man's back. Later pictures of Nancy conformed to the styles of the time, down to the dumpy gathered skirts and ballet flats of the 1950s. In the newest version of *The Clue of the Broken Locket* (1965), Nancy appears with the star of a rock group called the Flying Dutchmen. The young man (busy eluding groupies) wears a suit and tie and smugly short hair. Nancy has changed from a purified blonde to a titian-haired teenager—cute and not a day over eighteen. *The Double Jinx Mystery* (1973) shows Nancy and Ned in bell-bottom jeans, and Ned's hair is Beatle '65. Once upon a time even the villains wore ties.

Nancy Drew is virtually the lone survivor of a tradition which nourished several generations of adolescents. Once Nancy was a brilliant symbol of almost outrageous liberation. Now she is establishment— not a leader or pathfinder, but a cliché. The new emphasis on teamwork is odd and disconcerting. It's as if we were back where we started with the Outdoor Girls, as if we had not advanced to sisterhood but had regressed to the giggling girl groups and their tag-along boyfriends.

Nancy had liberated readers from that tyranny by 1930, but who is to liberate new readers from the established complacency of the Nancy Drew series? If Nancy is to live up to her image as a super-heroine, she must step beyond the old limits of her role and again advance into forbidden territory. That was the key to her success, and it could be reinvigorated—with Nancy or some new heroine altogether, a girl who does things and is good at them, regardless of what anybody says, someone who restores the 1930s promises of a determined, tough-minded sleuth. If there is to be a popular formula literature, which seems an inevitability, why can't it offer some healthful guidance and challenge? Once the girl detectives, in spite of their simplistic stereotypes, were inspiring because they did things they weren't supposed to, but there are no more of these rebel leaders. And even those were often written by women who wrote according to formulas created by men—they had to if they wanted to be paid for their work. There should be more opportunity now for women to write truly about growing up.

Perhaps because there are so few alternative heroines in series adventures, Nancy Drew's readership is spreading. But I suspect many modern adolescents are finding Nancy's exploits too superficial and her character too thin. This may be the central criticism, now that so many other complaints have been dealt with in the series. Nancy is just too straight. She is no longer doing the outrageous, but the obvious and expected. And the message in her stories is essentially the same as it always was: to give little girls the illusion that they can have their cake (and lollipops and Detective Burgers) and eat it too.

The indoctrination we have received from the girl detectives has been based on this paradox; they have thrilled us and contented us at the same time. Nancy gave us the conventional and the revolutionary in one compact image. Thus the influences have been both good and bad. I think it is wrong that the history books ignore the series, for they have played an immense role in the psychological history of this century's children. They have imbued them with dream-world expectations, within a formula of good and evil which barely skims the surface of character or experience. On the other hand, for children slow to read there may have been no better pleasure than the great banquet of endlessly thrilling series books. And for girls deprived of stimulating, accomplished role models, the girl detectives have held out a rare promise.

Notes

Chapter 1. Clues to the Girl Detective

1. My information about Stratemeyer Syndicate comes from these sources:

    (1) Arthur Prager, *Rascals at Large*, (New York: Double-day & Company, Inc., 1971).

    (2) *Contemporary Authors*, James M. Ethridge, Barbara Kopala, Carolyn Riley, eds. (Detroit: Gale Research Co., 1968).

    (3) Correspondence with Harriet S. Adams and Andrew E. Svenson at Stratemeyer Syndicate, East Orange, New Jersey.

    (4) "For It Was Indeed He," *Fortune*, April 1934.

2. Roger Garis. "My Father Was Uncle Wiggily," *Saturday Evening Post*, December 1964, pp. 64-67.

3. *Bobs, A Girl Detective* was probably not a direct source of Nancy Drew. It has been suggested that Mary Roberts Rinehart established a Gothic mystery pattern adopted by the Nancy Drew series. Rinehart wrote other types of novels for girls, including a remarkable little story, *Bab: A Sub-Deb* (New York: A. L. Burt Co., 1917), a long-buried feminist expression of frustration. The spirit of it is at the basis of the popularity of girls' mystery series. Bab's older sister is a debutante, and Bab is treated like a child until the sister is married off. Bab is more serious than her socialite sister, and wants to write and explore the soul. She reads a mystery novel about a girl detective: "In the book the Girl Detective had a small but powerful car, and she could do anything with it, even going up the Court House steps once in it and interupting a trial at the criticle moment." (P. 225) (The spelling is Bab's own.) Part of Nancy Drew's success was that she drove her own car. I have not attempted to trace the novel Bab reads—perhaps it is one of Rinehart's own—but it is evident that girls were interested in being detectives even then. Bab is inspired by the book she reads to buy her own car, and she also tries to solve a mystery, which backfires when the burglar she trails turns out to be Romeo eloping with Bab's sister. Bab turns her attention to tracking a German spy and setting up the Girls'

Aviation Corps. The style, format, and humor of this book have been captured in two remarkably similar modern stories, Sylvia Plath's *The Bell Jar* and Patricia Dizenzo's *An American Girl*.

Chapter 2. The Land of Milk and Honey Bunch

1. *Dick and Jane as Victims: Sex Stereotyping in Children's Readers* (Princeton: Women on Words and Images, 1972).

Chapter 3. Bobbsey Bourgeois

1. Russel Nye, *The Unembarrassed Muse* (New York: The Dial Press, 1970), p. 78.

2. Gypsies skulk in and out of juvenile fiction like panthers on the prowl. They are part of the apparatus of series books, a convenient symbol of all the aspects of evil which thrill and fascinate little escapists. One might suspect the stereotyped view of Gypsies was created by these books. Here you learn that Gypsies are swarthy and sneaky; they steal chickens and children; they hoard jewelry and wear bandanas and gold earrings; they travel in fancy wagons; and, being heathens, they won't work for a living.

Ruth Fielding gets waylaid by Gypsies and so do the Motor Girls, who have to fend off the "Gyps" in at least two books. The Bobbsey Twins and the Outdoor Girls encounter Gypsies in genuine Gypsy caves, and most of the girls' mystery and adventure series get around to Gypsy themes eventually. Ruth Fielding brings Gypsy crooks to justice—disbanding the tribe and exiling the Queen (a toothless hag) to Bohemia. Typically, there is one young Gypsy boy who stands apart and adopts civilized ways and succeeds in reforming his tribe. Ruth Fielding and her friends are fascinated with the philosophy of a Gypsy boy, a free spirit of the "pleasant country roads."

> The cities Roberto could not bear. "There is no breath left in them—it is used up by so many," he explained. He did not eschew work because he was lazy, it seemed; but he saw no use in it.

142

Clothing? Money? Rich food? Other things that people strive for in the main? They were nothing to Roberto. He could sleep under a haystack, crunch a crust of bread, and wear his garments until they fell off him in rags.

But he knew the woods and fields as nobody but a wild boy could. Every whistle and note of every bird was as familiar to him as his own Tzigane speech; and he could imitate them with exactness.

Ruth Fielding and the Gypsies, pp. 37-38

This wild nature boy gets turned on by capitalism the instant a kind American businessman promises to help him become an Alger hero. "That is better than trading horses—eh?" says Roberto. (P. 201)

The treatment of Gypsies in juvenile fiction hasn't changed to this day; good Gypsies are played off against bad ones, and they all wear gold earrings. A 1967 Dana Girls mystery, *The Secret of the Minstrel's Guitar*, uses the same theme. A dashingly dark minstrel exiled from his tribe for honesty helps reform the Gypsies. Gypsies run through these books like an exotic strain of wild violin music, a much more explicit expression of racism than the more taken-for-granted attitudes about Blacks which pervaded series books until recently.

3. The stories are written according to a very precise plan. Stratemeyer Syndicate notes in its listing of copyright dates for Bobbsey books: "Books published up through 1954 contained 25 chapters. The two titles published in 1955 contained 22 chapters. From 1956 on stories were cut to 18 chapters." Russel Nye also points out that Stratemeyer's original formula called for exactly fifty jokes per book, and either exclamation points or a question mark at the end of each chapter. (*The Unembarrassed Muse*, p. 77)

Chapter 4. Nancy Drew: The Once and Future Prom Queen
1. "For It Was Indeed He," *Fortune*, April 1934.
2. Lee Zacharias, "Nancy Drew, Ballbuster," unpublished paper, p. 40.

3. Professor James P. Jones made this observation in "Nancy Drew, WASP Super Girl of the 1930's," *Journal of Popular Culture*, Spring 1973.

Chapter 5. *The Secret of the Phantom Friends*
1. Some of the information in this chapter was obtained from correspondence and talks with Margaret Sutton.

Chapter 6. *The Glamour Girls*
1. From correspondence with Helen Wells.
2. Cecile Megaliff, *The Junior Novel* (Port Washington, N.Y.: Kennikat Press, 1964).
3. Quoted in Rhoda Amon, "Children's Books—The Plot Thickens," *Newsday*, September 2, 1969.
4. Ednah D. Cheney, ed., *Louisa May Alcott: Her Life, Letters and Journals* (Boston: Little, Brown, and Company, 1921), p. 85.

Chapter 7. *Impostor Tea*
1. *Publishers Weekly*, July 16, 1973, p. 101.
2. Correspondence with Harriet S. Adams, Stratemeyer Syndicate.
3. Ibid.
4. Ibid.
5. Ibid.

Series Books

Aunt Jane's Nieces. Edith Van Dyne. Reilly & Britton Co.

The Beverly Gray College Mystery Series. Clair Bank. Grosset & Dunlap, Inc.

The Blythe Girls Books. Laura Lee Hope. Grosset & Dunlap, Inc.

The Bobbsey Twins Books. Laura Lee Hope. Grosset & Dunlap, Inc.

Cherry Ames Nurse Stories. Helen Wells, Julie Tatham. Grosset & Dunlap, Inc.

Connie Blair Mysteries. Betsy Allen. Grosset & Dunlap, Inc.

The Dana Girls Mystery Stories. Carolyn Keene. Grosset & Dunlap, Inc.

The Honey Bunch Books. Helen Louise Thorndyke. Grosset & Dunlap, Inc.

Judy Bolton Mysteries. Margaret Sutton. Grosset & Dunlap, Inc.

Kay Tracey Mysteries. Frances K. Judd. Cupples & Leon, Co.; Garden City Books; and Berkley Highland Books.

The Motor Girls Series. Margaret Penrose. Cupples & Leon, Co.

The Moving Picture Girls Series. Laura Lee Hope. Grosset & Dunlap, Inc.

Nancy Drew Mystery Stories. Carolyn Keene. Grosset & Dunlap, Inc.

The Outdoor Girls Series. Laura Lee Hope. Grosset & Dunlap, Inc.

Ruth Fielding Series. Alice B. Emerson. Cupples & Leon, Co.

The Trixie Belden Library. Julie Campbell, Kathryn Kenny. Whitman Books.

The Vicki Barr Flight Stewardess Series. Helen Wells, Julie Tatham. Grosset & Dunlap, Inc.

The Feminist Press is a non-profit, tax-exempt educational and publishing group organized to challenge sexual stereotypes in books and schools and libraries.

We are engaged in a number of educational projects designed to re-examine the ways in which children learn sex roles and to further the teaching of women's studies in schools and colleges. Members of the Press are advising school systems about their textbooks and curriculum, and providing in-service programs for teachers. Through the Clearinghouse on Women's Studies, The Feminist Press offers to students, parents, and educators, much-needed, inexpensive feminist resource materials: a comprehensive guide to feminist curricular sources (including a bibliography of non-sexist children's books); teaching aids for elementary, secondary and college classes; guides to women's studies courses and teachers; and a quarterly publication, the *Women's Studies Newsletter*.

Our publications program includes a series of feminist biographies of women and a series of reprints of important though neglected feminist works from the past, as well as a series of non-sexist children's books.

A complete listing of our publications appears in our catalogue, available on request.

FEMINIST PRESS REPRINTS

The Yellow Wallpaper by Charlotte Perkins Gilman. With an afterword by Elaine Hedges

Life in the Iron Mills by Rebecca Harding Davis. With a biographical interpretation by Tillie Olsen

Daughter of Earth by Agnes Smedley. With an afterword by Paul Lauter

The Revolt of Mother and Other Stories by Mary E. Wilkins Freeman. With an afterword by Michele Clark

The Storm and Other Stories by Kate Chopin (with *The Awakening*). Edited with an introduction by Per Seyersted

FEMINIST PRESS BOOKS FOR CHILDREN

The Dragon and the Doctor by Barbara Danish

Firegirl by Gibson Rich, with illustrations by Charlotte Purrington Farley

Nothing But A Dog by Bobbi Katz, with illustrations by Esther Gilman

I'm Like Me by Siv Widerberg, with illustrations by Claes Backstrom

Coleen the Question Girl by Arlie Hochschild, with illustrations by Gail Ashby

A Train for Jane by Norma Klein, with illustrations by Miriam Schottland

GLASS MOUNTAIN PAMPHLETS

No. 1 *Witches, Midwives and Nurses: A History of Women Healers* by Barbara Ehrenreich and Deirdre English ($1.25)

No. 2 *Complaints and Disorders: The Sexual Politics of Sickness* by Barbara Ehrenreich and Deirdre English